Broadway Swings

Broadway Swings

Covering the Ensemble in Musical Theatre

J. AUSTIN EYER AND LYNDY FRANKLIN SMITH

Bloomsbury Methuen Drama
An imprint of Bloomsbury Publishing Plc

B L O O M S B U R Y
LONDON · OXFORD · NEW YORK · NEW DELHI · SYDNEY

Bloomsbury Methuen Drama

An imprint of Bloomsbury Publishing Plc

Imprint previously known as Methuen Drama

50 Bedford Square	1385 Broadway
London	New York
WC1B 3DP	NY 10018
UK	USA

www.bloomsbury.com

BLOOMSBURY, METHUEN DRAMA and the Diana logo are trademarks of Bloomsbury Publishing Plc

First published 2015
Reprinted 2017

© J. Austin Eyer and Lyndy Franklin Smith

J. Austin Eyer and Lyndy Franklin Smith have asserted their right under the Copyright, Designs and Patents Act, 1988, to be identified as author of this work.

British Library Cataloguing-in-Publication Data
A catalogue record for this book is available from the British Library.

ISBN: HB: 978-1-4725-9000-8
PB: 978-1-4725-9001-5
ePDF: 978-1-4725-9002-2
ePub: 978-1-4725-9003-9

Library of Congress Cataloging-in-Publication Data
A catalog record for this books is available from the Library of Congress

Typeset by RefineCatch Limited, Bungay, Suffolk
Printed and bound in Great Britain

Dedicated to the memory of two Broadway legends and mentors who were interviewed for this book: Choreographer/Performer/ Swing, Tony Stevens, and Stage Manager, Beverley Randolph.

Contents

Preface

I vividly remember receiving the phone call from Jim Carnahan's office that I was being made an offer for the out-of-town tryout of *Curtains* (a new musical). I was thrilled, until the Casting Director paused and said, "They're offering you the position of Swing." My heart sank, "Swing?!" I had never been a Swing. It's such a weird feeling, to be so excited, disappointed, and nervous all at the same time.

I didn't know where to begin, so I spent the next couple of weeks calling all of my friends who had been Swings. I remember sitting down with three of them for dinner (Eric Fogel, Halden Michaels, and Chuck Ragsdale) and asking them about their experiences. They shared their process, their charts, some words of wisdom, and some horror stories. I remember in that moment being so fascinated by this information, and also being completely overwhelmed, while learning all the responsibilities of a Swing.

I spent the next three years of my life as a Swing on *Curtains*. I'm not going to lie, there were some great "ups" (like having Rupert Holmes call me personally, after a show, to tell me what a great job I was doing and how much he respected my work) as well as some difficult "downs"—a couple of which I will share in the pages to come. During the first few months of the job, I thought, "No one understands what this is like." In fact you spend a lot of your time explaining exactly what you do for a living to people who have never even heard of a Swing before. But as the months went by, I would run into colleagues of mine and they would say, "OMG! You're working as a Swing? I was a Swing once, let me tell you a story!" I began to realize there were *a lot* of people who understood *exactly* what I was going through. They had been exactly where I was, fighting their way to learn how to do this job that has no codified training. I just wish someone had said, "Watch out for this, or when this happens you'll be glad you did things this way," or "Oh, just wait until your first Split-Track!"

I knew there needed to be some sort of book or guide on how to be a Swing. It was crazy that every Swing had to go through the same learning curve I did, and just hope they were surrounded by a Creative Team, Stage Manager, or Dance Captain that would guide them in the right direction. Most musical theatre training programs prepare students for every job in the business, except this one. I started researching how the role of a Swing first originated and putting into my own words the lessons I had learned over the past few years.

While working on *The Little Mermaid*, my second Swing job, I remember thinking, "If only I could find a writing partner who was a Swing, then we could work on this book together." And then I looked across the dressing room at Lyndy Franklin and actually shouted, "Of course, *Lyndy!*" Lyndy and I had met previously when we were working as Assistant Choreographers on a project together. I knew we would make a great team, and thankfully she agreed.

I am so glad, after all of these years, that this labor of love can finally be shared with the theatre community. I am equally as passionate about teaching as I am performing, so over the past ten years I have been working with my students, at NYU, CAP21, and now Pennsylvania State University, on all of the things I wish I had known before starting my career. I cannot tell you the number of times I have received a frantic email from a former student or colleague saying, "*Help*! I have just been hired as a Swing for the first time and I have no idea what to do!!!" Lyndy and I look forward to having this book available to artists who find themselves in that exact position. We also have been developing workshops and courses that will train the young artist to learn not only how to be a Swing, but also how to work as a Dance Captain, Assistant/Associate, Understudy/Stand-by and how to support Swings, when cast in the Regular Playing Company. It is an honor for us to pass on the knowledge we learned on the boards of Broadway to the next generation of Broadway performers and future Swings around the world.

J. Austin Eyer

One of my first big performing jobs was dancing in the Ensemble in the *Radio City Christmas Spectacular*, helmed by John Dietrich and Tim Santos. It was there, in the hallowed Radio City Music Hall, that I learned to admire and respect the Swings. I was never a Swing at Radio City during my three seasons there—but I wanted to be! To me, the Swings were the most experienced, most knowledgeable (and the coolest) people in the cast. I would watch them, in awe, as they took the "Great Stage," in the most precise and detailed show I've ever done, and never missed a beat.

My earliest Swing "training" came from Tim Santos, who was also our Dance Captain. I am not sure whether he saw the "Swing Brain" in me, or if I expressed an interest, but I can remember having impromptu Swing lessons in the rehearsal hall between shows where we would work on reversing Choreography, practicing different tracks, and talking about the tricks of the trade.

After my third year at Radio City, I booked my first Broadway show—as a Swing and Understudy. I was ecstatic to make my Broadway debut, but also to give swinging a try. And, I loved it! Getting to experience *A Chorus Line* as several different characters was so cool. And, those moments of getting "thrown on" or "saving the show," when many people were out, were such a rush. I also became Dance Captain—another thrill for me. That is not to say that I didn't also begin to recognize the hardships of the Swings. It can be quite a thankless job, full of anxiety and the feeling that you are in a constant state of proving yourself worthy.

While swinging *The Little Mermaid* together, Austin approached me about co-writing a book about the amazing and crazy career of Swings. I did not hesitate. We both knew a "how-to" book on swinging was much needed in our community. But beyond that, we wanted to give the Swings a voice! In a job where you are supposed to go unnoticed, it is nice to have a moment to tell your story. And because we know, all too well, that Swings can put in more than their fair share of blood, sweat, and tears into a show, without much recognition, we want to congratulate and *thank* the Swings for their contribution to Broadway and American Theatre.

I am so grateful for all my performing experiences, but especially for everything I learned as a Swing and Dance Captain. Now as a

Director, Choreographer, and Educator, I rely on those lessons, daily, and hope to pass on what I have learned, not only to the next generation of Swings, but also to the next generation of Actors, Directors, Choreographers, Managers, Audience Members, and anyone who loves the theatre. Swings are *vital* to the success of a long-running show. Notice them, respect them, appreciate them.

Lyndy Franklin Smith

Foreword

Anyone who has ever worked for me knows that I love Swings! I depend on my Swings—they inspire me. When I am creating a show, before I bring any of the other Actors into the room, I start with the Swings. The health of the show has been entrusted to them, so I want them to understand where the Choreography comes from, what motivated each step. Watching them internalize the Choreography allows me to see my work from a different perspective. The vocabulary of a show exists in its Swings—that is why they are so valuable.

Swinging is one of toughest jobs in the theatre, and one that rarely receives the attention and applause it so rightly deserves. My hope is that this book will change that.

What Austin and Lyndy have written is the definitive guide to the Swing experience. Whether you are still in school or you are auditioning for your tenth Broadway show, read what they have to say and learn more about your craft.

And for those of you who are reading this simply as a fan of theatre, I expect you will think a little differently next time you open your Playbill and find one of those little slips of paper telling you a Swing is on that night. I only wish you could stand in the wings when a Swing hits the stage—the energy and excitement backstage is thrilling.

There are so many opportunities for a Swing. You might enjoy simply doing the work, but you might also find yourself traveling the world and mounting new productions, or you could find yourself nominated for a Tony Award, like Brad Oscar in *The Producers*!

If you take one thing away from this book, let it be this—be good to your Swings. They are the real heroes of your show.

Susan Stroman

Acknowledgments

Our sincere thanks go out to the following people, without whom this work would not be possible:

Supporters and Contributors

Actors' Equity Association—David Westphal and Louise Foisy
The Producers of *Chaplin*
Volunteer Lawyers for the Arts (NYC)
Rob Ashford
Lyn Cramer
Frank DiLella
Jerry Mitchell
Michael Price (Goodspeed Musicals)
Beverley Randolph
Clifford Schwartz
Randy Skinner
J. Kevin Smith (Scene Partner)
Susan Stroman
Jeff Whiting (Stage Write)
Eric Woodall
Tara Young
and

Mana Allen, Perrin Manzer Allen, Sara Edwards, Cathy Eyer, Aimée Francis, Jim and Luanne Franklin, Colin Hogan, Amanda Johnston, R. Kim Jordan, Sheila Kenny, Mike Kirsch, Ian Knauer, Jack Lee, Paul Loesel, Mark Madama, Joanne Manning, Kari Nelson, Sarah O'Gleby, Dr. Pamelia Phillips, David Richards, Missy Singson, Jeromy Smith, Marilyn Tagert, Christian Thompson.

Interview Transcription

Michael Biren, Karen Hyland, and Megan Marod.

Cover Photo

Photographers: Sasha Scherlinsky, Ian Starner; Actors: Jessie Davidson, Miranda Gelch, Connor McRory, Liz Schmitz, London Sperry, Aidan Wharton.

Introduction

It's 7:30 p.m. in Times Square, New York City, New York. Theatre-goers and tourists crowd the streets and Broadway Marquees illuminate the sky. Under the lights of Broadway, inside a famous, historic theatre of the Great White Way, a voice calls out!

Good Evening Ladies and Gentlemen, this is your Stage Manager speaking, and this is your half-hour call. At this evening's performance, Sarah is out, with Megan on for her. Mark is still out on vacation, with Joe on for him. And, tonight Greg and Jeff are out, with Steven on for both in a Split-Track. Please check the Call Board for the scene breakdowns. Your conductor tonight is Jason Jones. This is your half-hour call, Ladies and Gents, half-hour.

And thus begins another night on Broadway. The words might be slightly different. The names may change. But, behind the Stage Doors of every Broadway show, Stage Managers have been giving this nightly speech for nearly eighty years. The audience is milling about, inside the theatre, finding their way to their seats. Meanwhile backstage, the performers are warming up, putting on makeup, and getting into costume. At this particular show, four of the regular playing Actors are out; perhaps due to injury, illness, or maybe even a vacation. But, the show must go on! So, the Swings have sprung into action. Reviewing their lines, blocking, and Choreography; refreshing themselves on the locations of their quick costume changes; they are ready to take the place of the Actors in absence, without missing a beat. The audience will applaud and cheer, not even realizing that any changes have taken place. That is the magic of Broadway . . . the magic of the Broadway Swings!

Michael X. Martin, a veteran of over twelve Broadway shows, once called them "Broadway's Navy Seals"—ready at a moment's notice to do whatever it takes to save the show. When the Ensemble is missing an Actor, these versatile, incredibly talented men and women fearlessly take the stage, fit into formations and vocal harmonies flawlessly, and do it all with that show-biz flair so that the audience is none the wiser.

But, let's not get ahead of ourselves here. What exactly is a Swing? Technically, according to the Production Contract of Actors' Equity Association (The Union of Professional Actors in America, Canada, and the UK), a Swing is "a non-performing member of Chorus who swings all or fewer than all Chorus performing in Chorus numbers in the production." Basically, a Swing is an Actor that does not perform in the show each night, but instead serves as the cover for the Ensemble members.

The position of Swing is not to be confused with the position of Understudy or Stand-by. Understudies are performers who cover Actors in Principal roles, the leading roles of the show. Understudies are often also members of the Regular Playing Company, but can be Swings as well. Another major difference is that any given Understudy in a Broadway show might cover up to three Principal roles, but the number of "tracks" (Ensemble positions) a Swing might have to cover is unlimited and can sometimes range into the teens and twenties for any given scene in a show. Stand-bys, like Swings, are not onstage every performance. Yet like Understudies, Stand-bys are responsible for covering Principal Actors. Confused yet? All in all, Swings, Understudies, and Stand-bys are, in a way, a Broadway show's insurance policy. If any Actor has to miss a performance, these three groups take over. This way, shows never have to be canceled.

Swings, Understudies, and Stand-bys are equally vital to the successful run of a Broadway show. However, this book will focus on the Broadway Swing. Occasionally, the three groups can mix and mingle and we'll touch on a few stories and anecdotes from other types of covers. But, our spotlight will shine most brightly on the Broadway Swings.

In fact, the real stars of this book are the Swings themselves. Over 100 Broadway Swings were interviewed for their thoughts on the subject, and their experiences in the trenches, covering everything from fish on skates to New York City gang members to dancing spoons. Their direct quotes are interspersed throughout this book, to either help illustrate certain points or offer a different perspective.

And we, your authors, bring you first-hand experience as well. As professional performers, both of us have been Swings, Understudies, and Dance Captains on Broadway. (Austin was a Swing and Understudy on both *Curtains* and *The Little Mermaid*, as well as a Swing and Assistant Dance Captain on *How to Succeed in Business Without Really Trying*. Lyndy was Swing, Understudy, and Dance Captain for the 2006 Revival of *A Chorus Line* and a Swing on *The Little Mermaid*.)

Interestingly, a majority of people interviewed (including Directors, Casting Directors, Stage Managers, Choreographers, and even the Swings themselves) felt that Swings are the "unsung heroes of Broadway." The job, while incredibly rewarding, can also be terribly thankless. Unlike for Stand-bys and Understudies, it is not required that it be announced to the audience or posted in the Playbill when a Swing goes on in a Broadway show (unless they are performing in a featured role of some kind). Indeed, many Producers prefer that the audience not know that anything is different, night to night. So, the Swings often go unnoticed, by the audience at least. And sometimes, the Swings may feel unnoticed by their own cast mates and colleagues. But, without the Swings, Broadway shows would simply not be able to survive their lengthy runs. Karl Christian (Swing on *Miss Saigon*, *Beauty and the Beast*, *Jumpers*), said, "I've often compared being a Swing to the electric company. It's a completely necessary service that everyone relies on. Once in a while, [when] there's a power outage, everyone remembers how vital the electric company is, but mostly your services go unperceived."

Once the stories of these Broadway Swings have been told and their joys, frustrations, moments of glory, hilarity, and despair have been heard, we hope that everyone will come to know and respect these skillful masters of their craft.

On with the show . . .

Some Terms to Know

Before we get started with telling you about the "ins and outs" of swinging, we thought it would be beneficial to define some of the terms we will be using throughout the book. Here is a handy reference guide.

10 out of 12   A type of rehearsal day, during the *Tech* period, when Actors are called to rehearsal for ten hours out of a twelve-hour period.

Associate Director/Associate Choreographer Person in a secondary or assistant role to the Director or Choreographer of a show. They are usually the ones who visit the production more often to give notes, maintain show integrity, and check on the cast. In the Director's or Choreographer's absence, they have authority.

Blocking   The places Actors stand and the actions they might perform while delivering their scenes. Once an Actor's blocking is established, it should be consistent so that all scene partners know what to expect and *Understudies* and *Swings* have guidelines for when they go on for that role.

Blocking Charts   Diagrams that display the locations of *all* onstage Actors, during one given moment of the show. Often, these charts also display set pieces being used at the time and are usually from an aerial perspective. There could be hundreds of *Blocking Charts* for one show, as each moment and formation change must be documented (also known as Charts or Stage Charts).

Call Board   Bulletin Board usually located near the stage door that contains important posted information for the Actors, including sign-in sheets, schedules, cast changes, updates, meetings, etc.

Choreography   Any dance steps that might be prescribed for Actors to perform during the course of the show.

Chorus   Another word for *Ensemble* used frequently in Actors' Equity agreements.

Cut-Show   A performance that has been cut down from its usual cast size due to multiple Actors' absences, resulting in *Split-Tracks*.

Dance Captain   Person responsible for maintaining the *Choreography* of a show. This includes running "clean-up" rehearsals, training new cast members, giving Choreography notes/corrections, and maintaining the *Show Bible*—the book filled with all the notations of Choreography and formations of the show. (See *Blocking Charts, Show Bible.*)

Downstage   As the Actors face the audience, the front part of the stage (toward the audience).

Dresser   Member of the Wardrobe Crew assigned to help Actors with costume changes during a performance.

Ensemble   *Chorus* members of a show.

House   Area of the theatre in which the audience is seated.

In-Out Sheet   Posting on the *Call Board* announcing which Actors are out of a particular show and which *Swings/Understudies* are in the show to replace them.

Orchestra Pit   Area in which the musicians for a show are seated to play—usually *Downstage*, between the stage and the first row of seats and often lowered so that the audience can see above them.

Places   Period of time just before the show is about to begin when Actors, Musicians, and Crew are called to be in their starting positions (or "places") in order for the show to commence.

Pre-Production   Time spent in the studio, prior to the official start of rehearsals, when Choreography is often created. The Choreographer may bring in Assistants, Associates, and sometimes *Swings* to help in the process.

Previews   Part of the rehearsal process following *Tech*, when tickets are sold to patrons, but the show is not officially "open." This is a time when changes may be made, based on audience feedback and reaction, during daytime rehearsals and then implemented in the evening's performance.

Principal   Leading Actor in a show.

Production Contract   The agreement negotiated between Actors' Equity Association and the League of American Theatres and Producers that governs the rules and regulations for most Broadway productions.

Put-In Rehearsal   A rehearsal for the purpose of "putting in" a new Actor to the show. These may be full run-throughs or quick moment-to-moment rehearsals for a *Swing* in a new track.

Regular Playing Company   Actors who perform regularly in the show. (Also may be referred to as First Cast.)

Show Bible   A book that contains all important information pertinent to the staging of a given show. This could include Script, Score, *Blocking Charts*, *Choreography* notation, *Tracking Sheets*, and any Director's or Choreographer's notes.

Split-Track   Term used when one *Swing* is covering two or more tracks in a given performance. The Swing will switch back and forth between the two tracks so that the most important elements of each track are covered for the performance. (The remaining, uncovered, elements of each track would then be "cut" from that particular performance.)

Stage Left   As the Actors face the audience, the left-hand side of the stage.

Stage Manager/Stage Management   Person/team responsible for managing all backstage activity during a show. This includes "calling" the show—communicating via headset with lighting, sound, and fly crew members who operate technical elements during the show; communicating with Actors; running rehearsals; handling the day-to-day management of backstage operations. Stage Managers are also responsible for maintaining the integrity (Director's original vision) of the show.

Stage Numbers and Stage Depths   Markings on the stage floor to help Actors evenly and accurately space themselves during a performance. Usually Stage Numbers start with Center Stage (marked at "0") then go out *Stage Right* and *Stage Left* in two-foot increments, denoted by even numbers on the stage. Stage Depths run *Downstage* to *Upstage* and may be denoted by markings. Or, Actors may guide off set pieces or wings/legs. (See *Wings.*)

Stage Right   As the Actors face the audience, the right-hand side of the stage.

Stand-by   Another form of *Understudy.* The Stand-by usually understudies one to two major *Principal* roles and is not a member of the *Regular Playing Company.*

Swing   Actor responsible for understudying the *Ensemble* of a show. The number of people they might be covering varies from show to show.

Tech   Short for Technical Rehearsal. Period of rehearsal time devoted to adding technical elements, including set pieces, lights, sound, special effects, and costumes to the work previously done in the rehearsal room. Tech is usually the first time the show is rehearsed on the stage, as opposed to a separate rehearsal studio.

Track   Term used to describe an Actor's individual responsibilities through an entire performance of a show. From start to finish, their locations onstage and tasks to perform at each location make up their "track." This is especially helpful to define *Ensemble* roles that may not have a character name associated.

Tracking Sheets   Device used by *Swings* to help keep track of each role they cover. Usually this is the long-hand version in which a Swing would write out exactly each location the Actor is in and what they are doing at that location, along with any additional important notes.

Understudy   (n.) Actor responsible for covering *Principal* roles in a show, usually limited to three to five roles. Often, the Understudy has a regular or featured role in the *Ensemble*, but can also be a *Swing*; (v.) To learn the part (dialogue, *Blocking*, music, and *Choreography*) of another Actor, so that in the event of that Actor's absence, the understudying Actor would be given the opportunity to perform the role.

Understudy Rehearsal   Weekly or bi-weekly rehearsals held for the *Understudies* and sometimes *Swings* to rehearse their roles. They usually occur onstage, but without any technical elements.

Upstage   As the Actors face the audience, the back part of the stage (away from the audience).

Wings   Space just offstage to the right and left sides, usually covered by curtains ("legs") that cover the Actors as they wait to make entrances or complete exits.

1

What is a Swing?

The History of Swings

In the earliest days of Broadway, the use of **Swings** was not common. The run of a show (the number of performances from Opening to Closing) was not nearly as long as it is today. From what we have heard from industry veterans, Actors may have missed fewer shows back then. Vacations and Personal Days were a thing of the future.

But, in the mid-twentieth century, Broadway shows began running longer and longer. The Actors' Union (Actors' Equity Association) also began to require that Producers allow Actors time off, after six months of continuous performances. Thus, having a small group of Actors, at the ready, to go on for injured, ill, or vacationing Actors, became a necessity.

According to our research in the Programs and Clippings Archive at the New York Public Library for the Performing Arts, the first recorded show retaining the services of a Swing was *Black Rhythm* in 1936, which is said to have employed one male Swing performer named Sinclair Brooks. The show ran for six performances. (We assume Mr. Brooks might never have gone on.) Following *Black Rhythm*, several other early shows hired Swings, including *Oklahoma* (1943), *Porgy and Bess* (1953), and *Peter Pan* (1954).

It is difficult to track exactly when the position of Swing was created. In the early years, many shows would use the **Dance Captains**, Assistant/**Associate Choreographers**, and other cast members to fill in necessary parts of the show if someone became ill or injured. It was not until the 1960s that Swings were mentioned in the **Production Contract**; and not until 1974 that Broadway shows (with a **Chorus**) were required to have Swings.

> In the old days, like the 1950s and 1960s, Equity wasn't so strict about rules. Most of the dancers would generally know all the choreography. You would be asked to fill in for someone on a certain section, and we would always accommodate. Then the word "track" crept in, and none of that is allowed now.
>
> HARVEY EVANS (*Damn Yankees,*
> *Sunset Boulevard, Oklahoma*)

(Note: Credits listed throughout the book are Swing credits only. Unless otherwise noted, the Swing is/was a member of the Broadway Company.)

It is also unclear as to whether or not Sinclair Brooks and his fellow Swings were actually called Swings. Some early shows listed Company members as "Dance Alternate," "Understudy Singers and Dancers," or "Ensemble Understudy." It seems that the most common practice from 1930 to 1974 was to use Partial Swings— members of the **Regular Playing Company** who could cover specific numbers in the show.

Generally, we have found that the history of Swings is mostly undocumented and unclear. Our hope, with this book, is to change that. We have covered all the information we could find from the first part of the twentieth century. But, we hope theatre enthusiasts of the future will be able to look back at this book and really understand who Swings are, what they do, and why they are so important to theatre history!

The Definition of a Swing

We asked all the Swings interviewed in this book where they thought the term "Swing" originated:

> I believe the term "Swing" comes from the fact that a swing on a playground goes from one side [to] the other seamlessly. In a lot of older Broadway shows the choreography was often separated

into two sides of the stage. A Swing could perform one side or the other without a problem whereas a regular chorus member who was used to performing on one side of the stage would have a very difficult time.

GREGORY GARRISON (*Beauty and the Beast*,
Jerome Robbins' Broadway, Me and My Girl)

I've always thought of it as someone who can swing from one part to another, like a monkey in the jungle. What's funny about it to me is that the word "swinging" seems to imply such fun and ease, when it's often the exact opposite!

LEAH HOROWITZ (*Thoroughly Modern Millie, La Cage Aux
Folles, Fiddler on the Roof, The Woman in White*)

There was something in World War II called "the swing shift"— basically when the men went off to war women stepped in for the men to do the work in the factories.

LARRY FULLER (Choreographer of seven Broadway shows;
Swing on *Funny Girl, West Side Story*)

Another theory that we heard is that the term "Swing" might have come from the days of Vaudeville and "Swing Acts." Supposedly, "Swing Acts" would be waiting in the **Wings**, in case another scheduled act did not show up for the performance, or if the show was running short and they needed another act to fill some time. No one really seems to know where, when, or by whom the term was coined. Regardless, it seemed to stick and is now an official title described in Actors' Equity Contracts and Rulebooks.

Today, most Broadway Musicals are required to retain at least one male and one female Swing. Many producers will use more, at the request of the Directors and Choreographers. (The norm seems to be two male and two female.) Generally, Broadway plays do not employ Swings, but use **Understudies** or **Stand-bys**.

According to the current Production Contract Agreement (effective 2011–2015), which covers most Broadway shows, Full Swings are contracted as Chorus members, but receive an extra stipend, currently 5 percent of their weekly salary. At the moment, there is no limit to the number of Actors a Swing may be asked to cover. We

know of Swings covering as few as three or as many as twenty
Actors (or **Tracks**). At any given performance in any Broadway show,
Swings may be filling in for **Ensemble** members. In fact, many
Swings end up doing six or eight shows a week, though they might
be on for a different person each night. There is no real limit as to how
many consecutive performances a Swing can perform in different
tracks. But, a Swing may not perform in the same Track for more than
three consecutive weeks (or up to four consecutive weeks, in the
case of sickness, injury, or disability).

Types of Swings

On Broadway today, there are four major types of Swings. The most
common Swing is the *Offstage Swing* or *Full Swing*. This Swing is at
the theatre every performance and has his or her own dressing
station. They remain offstage, unless called upon to cover for another
Actor. And, they are required to be at the theatre at the half-hour call
and remain until the end of the show. Some Offstage Swings may
be dismissed at a certain point in the Second Act, when it is deemed
too late to make it onstage if an Actor were to become ill or injured.
(Also, to note: If Ensemble members are also Understudies, the
Offstage Swings would go on for them, when they are on for their
Understudy role.)

A second type of Swing is the *Partial Swing* (or Internal Swing).
Partial Swings are Ensemble members who are actually onstage, in
the show, every performance. In addition to their regular performance
duties, they may also cover one or two other Tracks or featured roles.
When the Partial Swings move into another Track or role, sometimes
the Offstage Swing will then jump into the Partial Swing's position.
Or, the Partial Swing's Track may be cut from the remainder of the
show. (In terms of compensation, the current Production Contract
states that a Partial Swing would receive an extra $15 per week
stipend for these additional duties.)

A fairly recent addition to the Swing Family is the *Vacation/
Temporary Swing*. These Swings are generally not full-time employees
of the production. They are used when the full-time Actors in the
production take their one-week vacations (typically every six months).

Usually, when an Ensemble member takes a vacation, the Offstage Swing is on for that Track for the week, and the Vacation Swing takes the place of the Offstage Swing. Some shows do the reverse, and have the Vacation Swing on in the Ensemble Track, freeing up the Offstage Swing to cover for whoever else might be out that week. Vacation Swings may also cover when the Swings take vacation (yes, Swings get vacation too). And, Vacation Swings may also be brought in for an Actor's leave of absence or long injury. Some shows may choose not to hire additional Vacation Swings, at all. But, from the perspective of the Offstage Swing, that usually makes for a tough week. In this instance, there may not be enough actual bodies in the building to play all the tracks, resulting in **Split-Tracks** and **Cut-Shows**. (But we will get to that later.)

> Being a Vacation Swing requires more self-motivation than being a Full Swing because you have to find ways to keep the material fresh in your mind while you may be away from the show for several weeks at a stretch. As an example, when I was hired to Vacation Swing *Chitty Chitty Bang Bang*, I was hired for two weeks in June during which I was taught six tracks in the show. I created my Swing Book during these two weeks and then I was not hired for my first actual Swing week until sometime in August. The other difference in being a Vacation Swing is that you have no guarantee of employment. I was given a schedule of proposed weeks during which I would be used but that was constantly changing as people added or canceled vacations and injuries occurred. Also as shows start to struggle financially one of the first things to disappear is the Vacation Swing.
>
> JEFF WILLIAMS (*The Pirate Queen*, *Chitty Chitty Bang Bang*, *The Music Man*)

And, finally, there are *Universal Swings*. This type of Swing is used when there are multiple Companies of a production running simultaneously. For example, if a show has a Company on Broadway, two separate National Tours and a sit-down production in another major market (Chicago, Los Angeles, Las Vegas), they might need to employ a Universal Swing. This position works much like a Vacation Swing, except that this Swing would also travel from Company to

Company to fill in where needed. So, that Swing might spend three weeks with the Broadway Company, then be flown out to meet up with the tour for a couple of weeks, followed by a lay-off, followed by two weeks with the L.A. Company, etc. This position can be extremely difficult, as each Company is likely to have slight differences in staging, **Choreography**, or tracks. Also, the last-minute travel and the uncertainty of where you will be living next can take its toll. We have devoted part of Chapter 12 to this subject, so read on for more information. (It is also important to note that the term Universal Swing is not used in Equity Contracts. They are also referred to as Vacation/Temporary Swings. But it is a widely used term in the industry.)

All Swings, no matter their classification, are important to the success of a long-running show. Together with the Understudies and Stand-bys, they ensure that no matter what happens with the Actors, the show will go on!

2

Selecting the Swing

Now that we have covered the basics of what Broadway Swings do, let's discuss the life of a Swing, from Audition to Closing Night.

Getting the Job

It is not always easy being hired as a Swing, especially the first time.

> I wasn't happy at first. Like most young performers starting out, I automatically assumed that it meant the Creative Team did not think I was good enough to be onstage every night. It took being stressed out every day during rehearsals and having so much to learn, compared [with] the other people in the Ensemble, to realize that the Creative Team had a lot of faith in me. I realized that my training and hard work made me valuable.
>
> MEREDITH AKINS (*Mamma Mia!*, *Footloose*—Broadway and First National Tour)

Akins is not alone in her initial feelings of inadequacy upon being hired as a Swing. Part of this is due to the broad misconception that Actors chosen to be Swings and Understudies are not as talented as the Regular Playing Company. However, the truth is quite the contrary. Often, the job of the Swing requires even greater talent and skill.

> I *do* think there is the misconception that a Swing is a runner up to an Ensemble track. I partly understand where this comes from, in

the sense that there are many Swings who want to transition into Ensemble tracks or leading roles. The myth that I try to dispel is one of a Swing being a beginner or "try out" position. I am often having this conversation with agents who submit kids fresh to New York, with no prior Swing experience, as Swings, because they feel it could be a good way *in* for their clients. I sometimes feel that Creative Teams view Swings in the exact opposite way. To Creative Teams, the Swings have to be the *most* experienced, the *least* "green" performers in the show. Casting the Swings is one of the most important and most difficult aspects of putting a show together. The Creative Team has to trust that the show can run in the hands of the Swings. Swings begin to feel like an extension of the Creative Team. It is not a coincidence that many of our current Broadway Directors and Choreographers were once Swings.

ERIC WOODALL (Casting Director, Tara Rubin Casting)

It really takes a particular kind of performer to be a Swing. I believe fiercely that the Swings are generally the most talented and under-recognized kind of Actor. We are hired not for our specificity in look and voice and talent, but [for] our universality and adaptability of look, voice, and talent. We are not in show business to be stars, or to have the adulation and recognition (although those things are wonderful). We do what we do because we love what we do, and *can* do what we do.

JUSTIN GREER (*Anything Goes, The Mystery of Edwin Drood, Shrek, The Producers*)

What it Takes

The process of casting the Swings for a Broadway show is incredibly important and challenging. Many factors go into the decisions that a Director, Choreographer, or Casting Director makes regarding who will Swing any given show. Everything from type and look, to size and shape, and (of course) ability may be taken into consideration.

Broadway Swings today must also be tremendously versatile. In Broadway's Golden Era (and before), shows typically consisted of a dancing Ensemble and a singing Ensemble. There may have been separate Swing positions to cover each Ensemble. These Actors may have been called "Dance Alternate" or "Chorus Understudy." However, Broadway shows these days are characterized by a much smaller Ensemble, often made up of "triple-threats" (Actors equally capable in the areas of singing, dancing, and acting). Thus, the Swings must be "triple-threats" as well.

> I learned very early that [the Swings] were the most important people in the building. And also, quite frankly, my feeling is that they're usually the most talented.
>
> TARA YOUNG (Associate Director/
> Choreographer on ten Broadway shows)

> On the opening of *Bye Bye Birdie* I got a telegram from Gower [Champion] saying, "Congratulations for doing the most difficult job in the theatre!" And suddenly it all made sense to me! Yeah. Dammit! You have to be good!
>
> ED KRESLEY (*West Side Story, Bye Bye Birdie*)

In addition to their traditional craft, today's Broadway shows require Actors to hone many other skills. Actors and Swings are often asked to tumble, fly (aerial arts), skate, or play instruments. So, the best candidates for Swing positions are those Actors with many, sometimes hidden, talents.

Another important factor in casting Swings is type. Type is a general term that covers height, build, hair color, eye color, or even skin color or ethnicity. Type is an important part of casting every character in a show. But, for the Swings, it can be even more crucial. A Swing has to be able to believably fit into the Ensemble. Sometimes, this requires a show to hire a "tall Swing" and a "short Swing" so that the height of the overall Ensemble is not compromised when a Swing goes on. An example of this might be *42nd Street*. Often, the dance formations in a show like this are based on the heights of the Actors. If a line of ladies were placed tall to short, the Swings would have to fit seamlessly into several places on the line.

Other examples of shows where type would be of major importance could be shows like *West Side Story, Hairspray,* or *Ragtime*. In shows where the ethnic diversity of the characters contributes to the storyline, there must be Swings for each specific ethnic group. In *West Side Story*, for example, potentially separate sets of Swings may cover the Jets and Sharks. The Jets tend to be fairer skinned, while the Sharks need to appear (if not actually be) Hispanic. Thus, there must be Offstage Swings of each type in order to maintain the integrity of the show.

But, beyond look and skill set, perhaps the most important part of casting Swings is finding those with the "Swing Brain." This factor can be difficult to teach and is basically a combination of organizational skills, a "level head," spatial awareness, and a "go-with-the-flow" attitude.

Good Swings have an ability to understand choreographic vision. They can see the entire stage picture in their head, and where each Actor fits into that picture. They are chameleons. Swings must be able to jump from part to part easily. They must have a good command of technique in all disciplines, but also must be able to reverse dance combinations, sing any part in a phrase with harmonies, or perform any given line in a scene. Sometimes handling acting choices as a Swing can be even more difficult than memorizing harmonies and dance steps. As a Swing filling in for scene work, he or she must maintain the integrity and rhythm of the scene, while still finding a way to make the moment his or her own.

The ability to stay calm in stressful situations is also vital. Swings can find out at, literally, a moment's notice that they must go on. And in those fleeting moments of preparation, good Swings are able to block out the panic and nervousness and focus on achieving the task at hand. Creative teams can often sense this personality type and know that it is characteristic of a great Swing candidate.

Well a good Swing is someone who rolls with it. We're going to take the talent for granted. We are all professionals and we're going to assume that the Swings know the gig. And then it becomes about being someone who doesn't get flustered at fifteen minutes to places, when the call comes [that they have to go on]. And by the same token you want someone who is honest and says, "You know what, I don't know that yet. But, I'll do my best."

CLIFFORD SCHWARTZ (Stage Manager
of over thirteen Broadway shows)

An ability to prioritize, to learn quickly, to observe carefully and incorporate changes, to have a clear notation system for when you rehearse alone, a willingness to work hard, all topped off with a pleasant, calm personality. If you can do all those things, it creates a sense of confidence and competence and that goes a long way towards making the job easier.

MELANIE VAUGHAN (*Ring of Fire*, *Imaginary Friends*)

Usually they have to be more accomplished so they can cover [a] variety of tasks. If they are a singer Swing, they have a good vocal range perhaps more than some of the onstage performers. They also have to be able to dance at least some, because they will be going on as a second cover at some point. Conversely, a dancer Swing has to be a pretty good singer—perhaps better than some of the onstage dancers. I personally look for someone who is fearless and organized. Because they have to remember so much at a moment's notice that's critical. Their "cliff" notes need to be really well done. I've known some wonderful performers who aren't good Swings because they don't know how to be precise onstage.

BEVERLEY RANDOLPH (Stage Manager
of twenty-two Broadway shows)

Selecting the Swings (Swing Auditions)

In the initial audition process for a Broadway show, there are not usually separate auditions for the Swings. In fact, many Actors may find themselves at a final callback for a Broadway show, not even knowing that they are being considered for a Swing position. Sometimes, it also can happen that the Swings are not cast until the Ensemble has been cast; for, as we established, sometimes the Swings have to be somewhat based on the makeup of the Ensemble. In that case, there might be a separate Swing audition. Or sometimes, as Actors may be eliminated from the initial audition, they might be put into a "Swing pile" or "Swing folder," to be called back to the Swing audition.

In a general audition process, Swing candidates may not be asked to do anything differently from the rest of the Actors. In that instance, the Creative Team has to deduce who might make good Swings based on their performance in the audition.

I like to hold a Swing Audition. That's actually a really easy way—an Invited Call for Swings. Because then, the people that show up want to be there. And usually it starts off with who's swung before. We pull all those aside. But that doesn't mean that if they haven't swung before they couldn't get the job. You put people in a group of five— [and you look to see if they] stay in formation. If someone doesn't stay in their formation, they're not likely to follow orders well in a musical. And then I switch the formation to see if they can dance in another area of the room. If you don't dance in your formation, then I don't think you'd be a great Swing. And I always ask the Actor, "Do you like to swing?" they [might] pause for a second and say, "I will." Now, that doesn't mean that they couldn't be a Swing. But believe me, if I was choosing between the person that said "I love to swing!" and the one that said, "I will," who am I going to choose? If the show has tap in it, I would make somebody reverse the tap combination. And, I don't tell them I'm going to do it. I would say, "Now, reverse it." You can see the [potential] Swing. They're quick on their feet.

TARA YOUNG (Associate Director/
Choreographer on ten Broadway shows)

As far as auditions go, if I am specifically looking for a Swing, I keep my attention on who in the room has the ability to learn quickly. That quality in a dancer usually is pretty obvious and I pay specific attention to someone who might catch my eye and keep watching them to see if they achieve both the style and the technique of the combination. I might keep someone for more exploration and throw some other combinations and styles at them in a quicker fashion to see how they do. I also look for someone who is relaxed, focused, and able to go with the flow— all qualities that are needed in a good Swing dancer.

RANDY SKINNER (Choreographer
of five Broadway shows)

In a Replacement Audition (after the show has been open for a while and a specific Swing position needs to be replaced), the audition may be geared more toward specific Swing skills. By this point, the show has been created, rehearsed, and running for a while. The exact requirements of the Swing Track have been determined. In these auditions, the Creative Team and Casting Director are looking for someone who can fit the bill exactly. Candidates might be asked to sing a specific high or low note, do a specific dance step, or read some specific lines. This, along with fitting the mold of the Actor being replaced, contributes to who ends up winning the job.

> Swing auditions can be more layered. I have seen dance departments teach harder combinations in less time to see how fast the potential Swings pick it up. I have seen music departments test Swings in holding harmony parts. A potential Swing must pick up faster than other folks. They also have to retain multiple tracks.
>   ERIC WOODALL (Casting Director, Tara Rubin Casting)

As mentioned above, a factor in casting Swings can sometimes be previous experience. Some Actors on Broadway have been known to say "Once a Swing, always a Swing." Good Swings can be hard to find. Once Casting Directors and Creative Teams know of a Swing's proficiency at their job, they often want to re-hire them over and over in many shows. Thus, Actors having previous Swing experience on their resumé can be helpful.

> If I am auditioning for a show that I know is looking for Swings then I make a point of noting that I have swung several Broadway shows. If I am really hoping to be cast in the Ensemble then I don't list the Swing title.
>   GREGORY GARRISON (*Beauty and the Beast,*
>   *Jerome Robbins' Broadway, Me and My Girl*)

As Garrison points out, while some Actors love repeatedly being hired in the Swing position, others consider it a detriment. Many Actors feel they can be easily "pigeon-holed" as a good Swing, when they would really like to be in the onstage Ensemble from time to time. Because the talents and skills of a Swing are so specific, they are often more valuable offstage than onstage. The Creative and Management Teams need a deep bench of solid Swings to ensure the success of the show. For good Swings who want to be onstage, this can be just as frustrating as it is flattering.

> Once we have found good Swings, yes we are going to pursue them to swing again. It doesn't mean that we will only think of them as a Swing. A Swing is so difficult to find. We have often joked that it is much more difficult to cast the Swings than it is the Principal roles. There is some truth to this. The skill set required of a Swing is *huge*. When you find someone who can do all of that, it can sometimes be a shame to cast them in merely one track.
>
> ERIC WOODALL (Casting Director, Tara Rubin Casting)

> I list current experience on my resumé, whatever that may be. I understand that a stigma can be attached and that once a Swing/ Understudy/Stand-by, always a Swing/Understudy/Stand-by. Let's all work to break that stigma and be prepared to say "no" to a gig if you've had enough multi-tasking.
>
> MERWIN FOARD (*Aladdin*, *The Addams Family*, *Sweeney Todd*; total of over sixteen Broadway shows)

Swings must be versatile, smart, organized, and reliable and yet be able to roll with the punches and accept that they are more valuable offstage than onstage. Sound like a tough gig? You betcha! But, we are just getting started. And for all you Swings-to-Be reading this book, don't worry—we have a lot of helpful hints and "how-to's" coming your way to help you navigate this tricky, but awesome, job!

3

Swings in Rehearsal

In the rehearsal process, the job of the Swings is walking a fine line between staying out of the way of the Regular Playing Company, while at the same time observing their every move by learning alongside them. Directors and Choreographers will create the show with the Actors who will be performing every night. So, the Swings must remain on the sidelines. But, they must also be processing all of the information given to the Regular Playing Company and be ready to jump in, at a moment's notice, for any Actor they cover.

Studio Rehearsal

For an Original Broadway Company, a four- to six-week rehearsal process is pretty standard. The first few weeks take place in a rehearsal studio. During that time, the Regular Playing Company is creating their roles and tracks. The job of the Swings is to record the daily creations of the Company and Creative Team, learn everything, and begin to organize their notes in order to be prepared to go on at any time. This means every single dance step, all the vocal parts and dialogue, for each part they cover, must be memorized. And, the Swings may even go on as early as in the first few days of the rehearsal process.

In the rehearsal room I like to give the Swings a table to take notes. I also like to get the Swings into the rehearsal whenever someone is in a fitting or absent. Once I have the fitting list for the next day I let the Swing know they may be on in that number for that person.

CLIFFORD SCHWARTZ (Stage Manager of
over thirteen Broadway shows)

Sometimes, when Actors are pulled out of rehearsal for costume fittings or publicity events, the rehearsal must go on, and the Swings jump in, getting their feet wet for the very first time. (A good piece of advice for future Swings to note here is to keep an eye on the **Call Board**. Often, costume fittings and other reasons an Actor might miss rehearsal will be posted a day ahead of time. By being observant, Swings can buy themselves a night of preparation—and look that much better when they have to jump in the next day.)

Being in an original cast, there was lots and lots of sitting, sometimes on the floor in a very uncomfortable position, looking up at everyone, scribbling in your notebook. By the end of the day, the cast would be tired from standing, and I'd be tired from being all hunched over, and my hand would hurt from the writing. Sometimes I'd get to fill in for someone who had to step out for a while, and I loved getting to be in the action and learn the show on its feet with everyone else.

LEAH HOROWITZ (*Thoroughly Modern Millie*, *La Cage Aux
Folles*, *Fiddler on the Roof*, *The Woman in White*)

It can be overwhelming for Swings to start rehearsals for a brand new show. As they watch the ten or twelve Ensemble members they cover, it can be too much to try to absorb everything all at once. Herein lies the power of hiring a team of Swings. Often, the Swings may be assigned priorities within the Ensemble. For example, if there are eight Ensemble members and two Swings, each Swing may be responsible for four priority tracks and four secondary tracks. The two Swings must ultimately know every single Track, but can focus on their four priority tracks at first. Also, in this way, these two Swings can help each other by sharing notes and teaching each other the specific Choreography. Teamwork can help ease the anxiety of having to learn so much material so quickly.

A THOUGHT FROM LYNDY

We definitely employed Swing teamwork on *A Chorus Line*. In fact, on one of the first days of rehearsal, Jeffrey Schecter (who played the role of Mike) was injured and one of our Understudies, Mike Cannon, had to step in for him for almost all of the studio rehearsal period. Mike Cannon also understudied the role of Mark. But, it was difficult for him to learn that one, while rehearsing the Mike role every day. So, I helped him by taking notes on Mark's placement in formations, etc. A day or so after Jeffrey returned to the rehearsals, Paul McGill (who played Mark) suffered an injury. So, Mike then had to go on for him. Mike and I met at a gym before the rehearsal and went over the Track together. When our **Stage Manager** asked Mike how he learned the Track so fast, he told him about my notes and how we worked together. I think Mike Cannon's recommendation helped me land a **Dance Captain** job at *A Chorus Line* a few weeks later. It pays to be proactive!

It can also be to the Swings' advantage to start observing the rehearsal behavior of the Actors they are covering. If there is an Actor who seems to be running late or just in the nick of time on a regular basis or someone who is feeling ill or calls out sick in the rehearsal process, it could be an indicator of their performance behavior. This might be a Track to focus on as you may be going on sooner than later!

Another interesting element in rehearsing as a Swing for a new Broadway show is the constant change happening in the process. As a new show is being mounted, changes are being made on a daily basis. Steps are changed; songs are cut; scripts get edited. All the while, the Swings must keep up with all the new material for all the characters they cover. Many Swings have said that they keep all their notes in pencil and bring a *big* eraser!

The constantly changing aspect can push some people over the edge. They think they've "got it" and then it's cut or altered and they have to erase the mental tape. This is really asking a lot.
BEVERLEY RANDOLPH (Stage Manager of
twenty-two Broadway shows)

It's a nightmare. A new show is constantly changing, so there is no way to learn everything until the show is set. However, when someone is at a costume fitting and you are asked to fill in, no one can understand why you don't know where to go at every moment. "Oh, I'm sorry, these sixteen counts have changed ten times today, and I haven't quite gotten all ten changes for all eight people!"

GINA LAMPARELLA (*Dirty Rotten Scoundrels*, *Fiddler on the Roof*)

Replacement Swings

Rehearsing as Original Cast Swings of a new Broadway show can be overwhelming and involve enormous amounts of work. But, coming into a show as a Replacement Swing can sometimes be an easier task. Often by this point in the process, the show has already been notated by the Swings as well as the Dance Captains and **Associate Directors** and Associate Choreographers. Most Dance Captains will let the Swings use their **Show Bibles** as a reference or even let the Swings copy their **Blocking Charts**. Instead of just learning by watching, the Dance Captains (who are well versed in each Track) often will lead the new Swings through the show, teaching them one Track at a time until they have learned all the tracks they are responsible for. In some cases, Dance Captains may teach a few tracks and major elements of the show and the Swings must pick up the rest by watching the actual performances of the already running show. One downfall to this can be the other responsibilities of the Dance Captain during that rehearsal period. If the Dance Captain is putting multiple people in the show or is called in to perform, those rehearsals may be more sporadic or even cut short.

A THOUGHT FROM AUSTIN

Having been a Replacement Swing a couple of times, I have found that while learning a show I always hit a "saturation point." Usually, Stage Management's goal is to teach a Swing about three tracks in the first two weeks. There are usually a couple of priority tracks that are learned first. After that the Dance Captains will help you get a couple more under your belt. And, eventually you work on learning the rest of the tracks on your own. Basically, the first two months as a Replacement Swing are spent learning Track after Track after Track. And during this time, there usually comes a point where your Swing brain becomes totally saturated and will stop processing any new information. It will be time to take the next step, jumping into a performance and making the mistakes needed, in order to learn more about the Track (and the show).

A suggestion: If a new cast member (male or female) happened to join the cast during my first few months with a show, I always asked to join them in the rehearsal room as a silent observer. That way, I could learn a new Track slowly with them (even if I didn't cover the Actor), work on partnering, or go over my spacing in relationship to the Track being taught. I would often learn a long list of unexpected things about the show, if I was allowed to attend these rehearsals.

Notation

While learning the initial tracks and maintaining all the changes, Swings must also start to work on their notation for the show. This enormous amount of work creates some pretty long days for the Swings. The regular rehearsal period for a Broadway Show is from 10:00 a.m. to 6:00 p.m., six days a week. But, most Swings will tell you that they spend most or all of their downtime working on the show. With the arduous task of absorbing ever-changing information for several people, Swings usually find themselves eating, sleeping, and breathing their show.

The Swings' notation process is, perhaps, the most important element of their preparation. The notes that they create through the rehearsal process are what they will rely upon to remember every last detail of each Track. When covering a grand total of ten or fifteen people, it can feel humanly impossible to keep all those tracks in your head. (Well, some Swings might disagree with us on this.) For the most part, Swings keep written records of the tracks they cover. It can be weeks, or even months, down the road before a Swing may go on for a given Track and creating these notes will be their most important tool.

There is no rule or right way to keep notes as a Swing. In fact, while interviewing Swings for this book, it was fascinating to find the numerous methods Swings are using. Also, the amount of notes they keep can vary. Some Swings need every detail written into their notes. Others jot down key moments and keep the rest in their head. The most important thing is for the notes to make sense to the Swing who is using them. When it is five minutes until the start of the show and the Swings find out they are on, their notes must be easy to read, understand, and quickly absorb.

Here are some common methods:

I have a master book with everyone in it on 8 x 10 sheets in a binder. Then I buy a 4 x 6 coiled index card book for each Actor I cover. Sometimes I will buy two for each person and separate Act I and Act II. In the little books, I make mini charts of the stage and just put the pertinent information down for only that Actor and their show. (Entrance, exits, props, costume changes, timing, crosses upstage or downstage of other Actors, numbers to be on and depth, etc.)

JENNIE FORD (*An American in Paris, Evita, All Shook Up, Urban Cowboy, Hairspray, The Music Man*)

I usually have full stage charts to start off scenes and dance pieces. I'll use arrows and lines to show blocking movements or choreography. I may use several charts for dances. I write everything out in a notebook as well. Once the show is set, I use index cards. Each track is a color, and I abbreviate their track scene by scene, noting entrances, exits, costume changes . . . it's sort of Crib Notes for Swings. The index cards fit neatly into a block size wooden cigar box that lives at my [dressing] station. When I am on for someone, I can pull out those cards, and I have even been known to tuck them into prop purses or costume pockets.

CYNTHIA LEIGH HEIM (*The Music Man, The Scarlet Pimpernel, Evita*—National tour)

I prefer Tracking Sheets and cheat sheets. I usually had a little notebook I carried around with me that had the tracks in them. Once you learn a show you know exactly which parts you have trouble with and you can reference that specific part of a person's show. I think it's hard to stay organized as a Swing, so the less papers you can have everywhere the better. I also used notecards at one point, but they are too small for me. I prefer notepads.

ALEXIS CARRA (*Wicked, Sweet Charity*)

A THOUGHT FROM LYNDY

In some shows, the cast doesn't leave the stage for long periods of time. Therefore, the Swings must do a great deal of memorization of their tracks. This was the case in *A Chorus Line*. Once the show begins, the next opportunity to step offstage to review notes is not until about thirty to forty minutes into the show when Diana sings "Nothing." So, you have to make sure you have memorized everything up to that point, and then again until Cassie's "Music and The Mirror"; and then from the company re-entrance after Paul's monologue until the end of the show. I did not make Notecards for this show since I could not reference them often throughout the show. Rather, I used my Tracking Sheets and made sure I had each section memorized before I hit the stage.

The introduction of new technologies has helped Swings with notation. Jeff Whiting's creation of Stage Write, an iPad app, is an incredibly helpful tool for Swings. With Stage Write, Swings can quickly and easily organize notes and create charts, all within a portable device. For all you Swings-to-be out there, be sure to check out the Stage Write information in Chapter 8, along with more detailed information from the Authors on how to notate and create charts.

I can now, with the [Stage Write] app, zap [charts to Swings] via wi-fi, and we're all on the same page. I basically keep the charts and I keep them up to date as we're in Tech, making small changes, and at the end of every day I send them the latest version, and they replace it on their iPads or computers. And the Swings ask me, "Could you put this detail on it for me?" So, I make a note on the chart there. And that way, it's all in the same place. It really is a collaborative effort. So it allows the Swing to really focus on, "OK,

I'm going to learn the movement and I'll figure out my piece and I'm not going to worry about writing it down."

JEFF WHITING (Choreographer/Director;
Associate Director on over four Broadway shows;
Developer of Stage Write Software)

As the Swings indicate, one of the most common methods of notation is *Charting*. This is a similar technique to what Dance Captains and Associate Choreographers create in order to record and preserve the show. Generally, a chart represents a given stage picture that includes set pieces, Wings, tracks, and **Stage Numbers**. The charts usually are marked with Xs for each person and can be labeled with character names, Actor names, Actor initials, and can sometimes be color-coded. Some Swings also add arrows or direction markings to show how the Actor got to the spot shown on the chart, or where they are going next. The "traffic" between formations can often be the most difficult part for Swings, so knowing who moves in front of or behind whom is very important.

Another method is creating a *Track Sheet* (or **Tracking Sheet**) for each Actor covered. Some Swings base these on their charts. Others

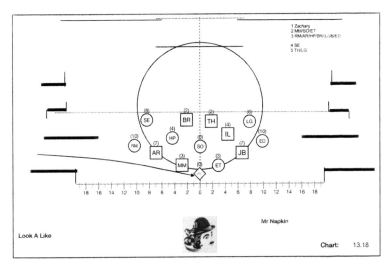

FIGURE 1 *Basic example of a chart, created using the Stage Write app.*

A Swing's Life- The Fictional Musical

M1 TRACK - Eric Fogel (EF- Green- Tenor)
Pre-Show: warms up onstage, runs popcorn jumps with Colin around ½ hour
Wig Call Time: **wig at 7:45 (Jeff)**
Dresser: Eric R.

Opening - "Got a Lot of Swinging to Do":
Costume: long jacket, no hat, **remember to put on glasses!**
Props: pick up newspaper SL prop shelf
Lines/Cues: *"Who will learn all those steps?"*...I will! I've been watching that track for weeks. *"Are you sure...we are all relying on you!"*...I'm a Swing, it's my job!
Partner: Karen "X jumps", Lisa 2nd half and "around the world"

- Preset onstage - in line with second leg - LF arm sequence
- X jumps on SL 2 with Karen (less force with lift), btw Richard-SL and Greg-SR
- Take out newspaper from LF pocket on "Get out", X center for lines (slow down)
- Look for yellow spike mark to stand for "jazz hands" section, sway LF
- Wedge: SR 3, David-SL and Greg-SR, follow Chuck to pinwheel
- Pinwheel: Go first, Megan-SL and Lisa-SR, move on count "4" step on **RH foot**
- Fancy Feet Section: "1-4" kick ball change, "5-8" RH LF RH pulse, bounce 8xs
- Peel off: go **SR** and follow Aimee (travel US of Lisa and DS of desk)
- Partnering section SR 9 with Lisa (remember to land on DS track, grab wrist instead of forearm)
- Around the world to the LF - in line with 2nd aisle - guide to center
- Button: LONG way to run to SL 3. End on DS track, cradle jump into split

Exit: Out SL2 on blackout (Look out for Matt)

Costume Change: (2:05 minutes) SL stairwell, into executive suit (keep glasses), shoes off first, then Margo will hand you black socks, suspenders, and vest.
Dresser: Margo

Scene 2 into "Swing on Over Here"
Costume: Executive suit
Props: Flowers (during number), strikes LF totem pole and all hats
Lines/Cues: *"..we're a hit."* Well of course, what did you expect? - Tenor solo: I've learned all the lines.
Partner: Colin - overhead flip

- Pop up first on count "2" - Muscle pose with RH arm
- Grab flowers from SR crew guy (Paul) - WATCH OUT for Richard-DS
- First formation: SL 8 David-SL and Mike-SR

Austin Eyer and Lyndy Franklin - 1/12/2015

FIGURE 2 *Example of a Swing's Tracking Sheet.*

skip the charts altogether and go straight to the Tracking Sheet. In this method, the entire show for one particular Track is written out—start to finish. This is often done in a prose method, as opposed to pictures and diagrams. The Swing may include very detailed information including what props to bring on- or offstage, where and when their costume changes take place, what part of the song to sing, etc. Often, the Swings who prefer this method adopt the "one track at a time" approach when learning a show. If trying to see the whole stage picture is too overwhelming, starting with one Track can ease the process.

A third method is *Notecards*. Having a ring of 4 x 6 index cards to carry backstage or tuck into your costume can be a great idea. Typically, Swings use the spiral bound cards, or punch a hole in the top of the cards and loop them through a key ring. This keeps all the cards for one Track together. On these cards, Swings will write notes similar to the Tracking Sheet, or may put "mini-charts" on each card. Having all their notes for a specific Track on a small, portable set of Notecards can be useful. They can be stashed at dressing stations for quick changes, easily carried around during rehearsals, and fit nicely underneath costumes, if need be (although they would never be pulled out onstage, of course!).

Stage Numbers

In this mathematical approach to theatre, many Swings rely on the use of Stage Numbers (sometimes called a "number line") for their **Blocking** bibles, charts, or Notecards. Stage Numbers are commonly used in theatrical productions and are just that—numbers placed on the front edge of the stage. Usually "0" marks the center of the stage and the numbers go up from there, both right and left of center. Actors use these numbers to help them go to the same place each time they do a scene or dance number. And the Stage Numbers can be extremely effective in high-traffic shows or shows with lots of automated set changes as the use of them keeps the performers consistent and safe from danger of moving people or set pieces. However, not all shows use a number line. Some use colored lights. Others do not use marks at all. Especially in those cases, Swings may

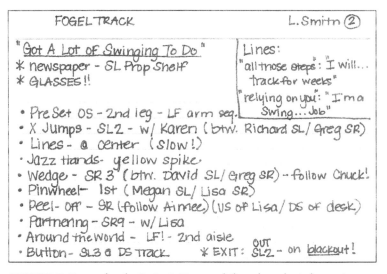

FOGEL TRACK   L. Smith ②

"Got A Lot of Swinging To Do"   Lines:
* newspaper - SL Prop Shelf   "all those steps": I will...
* GLASSES!!   track for weeks"
                                                  "relying on you": "I'm a
* Pre Set OS - 2nd leg - LF arm seq.   Swing... Job"
* X Jumps - SL2 - w/ Karen (btw. Richard SL/ Greg SR)
* Lines - @ center (slow!)
* Jazz Hands - yellow spike
* Wedge - SR 3 (btw. David SL/ Greg SR) - follow Chuck!
* Pinwheel - 1st (Megan SL/ Lisa SR)
* Peel - off - SR (follow Aimee) (US of Lisa/ DS of desk)
* Partnering - SR9 - w/ Lisa
* Around the World - LF! - 2nd aisle
* Button - SL3 @ DS Track   * EXIT: OUT SL2 - on blackout!

FIGURE 3 *Example of a Swing's Notecard (based on the information from the Tracking Sheet in Figure 2).*

find themselves using set pieces or other physical landmarks to help them know where to stand.

> *Spelling Bee* was performed on a thrust. No stage numbers were provided. The set was a gymnasium where the "Putnam Piranhas" played. In certain songs/scenes, I knew to stand (for example) on the third tooth of the piranha painted on the floor.
>
> TODD BUONOPANE (*The 25th Annual Putnam County Spelling Bee*)

I had one show that had different colored lights instead of numbers. There were about five colored lights on each side of center. It was similar to how we mark [with Stage Numbers], but a little less precise. I usually prefer more precise especially with larger casts. It is important for safety issues too when dealing with moving set pieces, turntables, or drops from the sky. As the show morphs a little, accurate placement systems can help solve problems for Actors such as "Why am I almost getting hit by the set piece coming in?" You can look back at the numbers *and* depths and say

"Well, you used to be upstage further above wing three when the set piece came in."

JENNIE FORD (*An American in Paris, Evita, All Shook Up, Urban Cowboy, Hairspray, The Music Man*)

I have performed in shows where there are stage numbers and depths and those without. I find the numbers to be very helpful but rely on other cast members' spacing to guide me as well. You can be on your "mark" and dancing on top of someone else, which is not good for the performers as well as the audience members.

GREGORY GARRISON (*Beauty and the Beast, Jerome Robbins' Broadway, Me and My Girl*)

As a Swing I think that the more precise the blocking is, the better you can do your job of slipping into someone else's show. I always think that my most successful days on are when at the end of the show someone will say to you "Oh, I didn't even know you were on today." That meant that the show flowed as it usually does. In *Jerome Robbins' Broadway*, the numbers and spacing [were] *not* as specific as you might imagine with all of the complex choreography. It demanded that the entire cast work like a real dance company and you had to constantly adjust your spacing and dancing to accommodate whoever was on that particular day and whoever your partner happened to be.

MARK S. HOEBEE (*Victor/Victoria, Beauty and the Beast, Nick & Nora, Jerome Robbins' Broadway*)

Highlighting

In addition to knowing where you go onstage, Swings also have to know what to do when they get there. And many Swings make these notations within their script, to have a sense of continuity. Often, Swings might cover every part in a given scene, and need to know every line of dialogue. Keeping "who says what" straight in the Swing's mind is crucial and takes an additional method of notation—*Highlighting*.

Most of the other notation we have discussed occurs on separate documents from the script and/or score, but sometimes notes need to be made within them. When covering multiple tracks or roles, a color-coded highlighting system can be helpful. This way, as you are reviewing your script or score, there is no confusion as to which person says or sings which line. This can be extremely helpful with harmony parts. Highlighting different notes in different colors can help Swings remember which line they are singing.

For those who might be covering multiple **Principal** roles, or characters with multiple lines or vocal parts, it can also be helpful to ask for multiple copies of the script or score. If highlighting every role in one script seems overwhelming to the eye, having separate scripts for each part covered can be a good solution.

I highlight each role in a different color . . . pretty standard I think. But then that can freak me out as I thumb through the script, I see how much I really am responsible for. I've recently started only highlighting the first few words on each line of dialogue straight down the margin. Not only does it look like less material, it saves on highlighter ink. Especially with original scripts, as new pages are coming every day!

MERWIN FOARD (*Aladdin, The Addams Family, Sweeney Todd*; total of over sixteen Broadway shows)

I used to color-code, but that got really old really fast. Once you learn the story, the lines are almost second nature, like the choreography. I usually incorporated any lines (singing or speaking) into the person's track sheet in my Swing bible, so I never really referenced the script all that much.

ALEXIS CARRA (*Wicked, Sweet Charity*)

A THOUGHT FROM AUSTIN

For *How to Succeed*, nine out of the ten tracks I covered had featured Ensemble roles, meaning they had a number of lines, which I was expected to learn in a matter of two weeks. I typed up and printed out the lines for all of my guys (plus the cue lines) and then pasted them onto Notecards so I could easily run them on the subway, or ask a fellow cast member or friend to run lines with me. Once I had memorized the lines, it was still great to have them as a refresher when needed.

4

The Next Step:
Tech Rehearsal and Previews

Tech Rehearsals

Once an Original Broadway cast has finished their Studio Rehearsal period, they move into the theatre and begin the Technical (or **Tech**) Rehearsals. In the Tech process, every scene and production number is blocked on the stage. Also, technical elements including set pieces, lights, and sound are added. Actors begin to wear their costumes and wigs, as they are ready. And the Tech process culminates with Dress Rehearsals, running the entire show from start to finish.

For the Swings, the Tech Rehearsal period can be a tedious time. While the Regular Playing Company is up onstage, discovering how it feels to work in costumes with sets and lights, the Swings are often at a table in a dark **House**, watching and wondering what it is like to be up there. As the technical elements are added, more changes are made. The Swings are furiously trying to capture all the changes for their notes and are often using this time to create or work on their charts, Tracking Sheets, or Notecards.

Tech Rehearsals can also be a slow process and Swings have to stay on task and use this time wisely. Some Swings may find that the slow, repetitive nature of these rehearsals can actually be helpful. They can watch numbers over and over again, to help with memorization and/or notation. If Swings know that a number is going to be run multiple times, it is a good idea to watch from different locations. For example, watching the first time from the tech table, the second time closer to the stage, and the third time from the balcony.

Sometimes, too, the Swings can feel a little forgotten in Tech Rehearsal. Though they are not onstage or an active part of this rehearsal, in the best case, they are given their own table and lights in the House and a place to plug in computers, so that they can continue with their important work to prepare for the show.

The Tech Rehearsal period can last anywhere from two to four weeks. The longest days (for both the Regular Playing Company and the Swings) are called **10 out of 12s**, during which the Company is called to rehearse for twelve hours, with a two-hour break.

During the Tech for *A Christmas Carol* at Madison Square Garden the first year, the Swings had some dedicated tables right near Stro [Susan Stroman] and we were in the middle of tech. We arrived one day to find our lights had been taken by someone to be used somewhere else. Susan didn't know this until rehearsal was well under way and I couldn't access some material she needed. Well, she got on the "god mic" and called the Tech to a stop. She asked for the house lights and said that the Tech would not continue until lights had been restored to our table. She said that the work that the Swings were doing at that table, cataloging the show and learning our tracks was just as important as anything that was happening onstage. It took about fifteen minutes for the situation to be corrected and then the Tech resumed. I have never forgotten that and I carry the respect she showed us with me as I approach every project.

MARK S. HOEBEE (*Victor/Victoria,*
Beauty and the Beast, Nick & Nora,
Jerome Robbins' Broadway)

I loved watching the Creative Team work. Being able to sit in the house and listen to the conversations of why a light should be green instead of red is something everyone should experience.

SEAN MacLAUGHLIN (*Lestat, Woman in White*)

The Tech process can be difficult because spacing, props, dance numbers, and songs get changed right on the spot. It usually happens right when you have told someone how proud you are of yourself now that your Swing notes were almost done. Nope! I found that my "final draft" of Swing notes were not done for a couple of months after we opened.

MEREDITH AKINS (*Mamma Mia!*,
Footloose—Broadway and First National Tour)

It's also a time when you start to feel quite removed from the rest of the cast and the show itself, but it is a good time to bond with the other Swings. I also find it important to do something physical during my dinner break—either go to the gym or for a serious walk—otherwise I am truly useless by the end of a long day of Tech. The true danger of Tech is that people always leave food on the Swing table—bags of chips or boxes of cookies—so it's very easy to gain weight through a two to three week tech!

JEFF WILLIAMS (*The Pirate Queen*,
Chitty Chitty Bang Bang, *The Music Man*)

Smart Swings will take advantage of the break periods during Tech to catch up on a little stage time. Usually during Tech, the Company and Crew will work in eighty-minute increments, followed by a ten-minute break. That break can be a golden opportunity for the Swings. During the break, the stage is vacated and (so long as **Stage Management** gives clearance) the Swings can actually hop up on the stage and start to get a feel for what their show will be like in the actual playing space. Granted, the work lights will be on and the Swings will likely be in rehearsal clothes, but this will be the closest chance they get to their own Tech process.

A THOUGHT FROM LYNDY

I remember just dying to get on the floor during rehearsals for *A Chorus Line*. Our team of Swings and Understudies worked really well together and we would usually rehearse together on the breaks. I remember once during Tech, we all started practicing the "Fourth Montage" during a ten-minute break. We got through the entire number and by the end the whole cast was clapping and singing along with us. We also used to get to rehearsal early and stay late (as long as Stage Management would let us) just to get a chance to work on the stage. You really have to be diligent to make sure you feel prepared!

Swings can also use Tech to watch from the Wings (if Stage Management allows), especially if numbers are being run multiple times. This can give the Swings a chance to dance in the Wings and keep the Choreography in their body. If new Choreography is being taught, sometimes Swings may be allowed to go onstage to learn and can then disappear again when it is time for the Creative Team to see formations, minus the extra Swing bodies. Again though, it is important to note that Swings should not be onstage or in the Wings during Tech without permission from Stage Management, for safety purposes.

Swings will not participate in the Tech Rehearsals onstage (unless an Actor gets sick or injured during the Tech period). While the Regular Playing Company has hours upon hours to get comfortable in their costumes, feel the lights on their faces, check their visibility and get used to the topography of the set, the Swings will never have this chance. For the Swings, the first time that they go on in the show will likely also be their first time in costumes, hair, and makeup, with lights, sets, and the full orchestra. (No pressure.)

A THOUGHT FROM AUSTIN

It's a good idea to find a time to check in with Wardrobe to see if any of your shoes have arrived. I would "check out" my shoes from the Wardrobe Head and wear them around the theatre to break them in. (I did the Tech for *Curtains* alternating two pairs of cowboy boots.) Once the show was up and running, I would then ask to set up a time to come in early to put on my costume or specialty pieces and then run the Choreography a couple of times so I could get a sense of what it feels like *before* I am on.

As several of the Swings we interviewed point out, another challenge during Tech is keeping up with the myriad of changes being made. Spacing, entrances, even bits of Choreography can be changed during this time. And the Swings have to be aware of all of it . . . for everyone. This can be especially challenging when changes are being communicated primarily to the Regular Playing Company. It is no fault of the Directors, Designers, or Choreographers. Their focus is getting the show up and running as quickly as possible. But sometimes, things get lost in translation and the Swings have to play catch-up to make sure everyone is on the same page.

Sometimes, just as they are about to give the cast new information or a change, Choreographers or Directors might turn the "god mic" off and start speaking normally to the cast. Swings may find themselves running quickly to catch the information (amassing bruises from the theatre seats along the way). This is the perfect time to develop eavesdropping skills. Swings should try to follow what is going on in the theatre at all times. Dance Captains and Associates will try to make sure everyone stays on top of the changes. But, at times, it can be everyone for themselves. Swings should take a notebook wherever they go, and not be afraid to say, "What were you guys discussing? Is there a change I should know about?"

Previews

Once the Tech process is completed and final Dress Rehearsals have come and gone, it is time to add the most variable element of the show—the audience. This period is called **Previews**, as the show is not officially open, but paid performances have begun. Also, during Previews, the show is still in a constant state of flux. The cast is still rehearsing during the day and changes are being made sometimes on a daily basis. The show does not get completely set or become "frozen" until Opening Night. (And by the way—things will still change even when "frozen.")

[Previews] can be very frustrating because you are not on at all, or it can be exhausting and frustrating because you are on all the time and can't really get your charts or organization done. Pick your battle. It's just not an easy time for a Swing, period (probably the hardest actually). So it's a time you have to maintain perspective and band together with the other Swings to stay sane!

ALEXIS CARRA (*Wicked, Sweet Charity*)

During *The First Wives Club* [Out-of-Town Tryout], one of the Ensemble women I covered (who also plays a very featured role) injured her ankle during the last week of Tech and the first week of previews. So, I was on. Zero rehearsal. It was actually a great way to learn the show. So nice to sort of "break in" the stage as a Swing. I was very thankful for it.

JENIFER FOOTE (*On the Twentieth Century,*
The Mystery of Edwin Drood, Rock of Ages,
A Chorus Line, Dirty Rotten Scoundrels)

A THOUGHT FROM AUSTIN

A helpful hint for dealing with all of the changes during Previews is to occasionally check in with the Actors you are covering, to see if anything major has changed that you might not have caught. Another suggestion is to ask the person who regularly performs the Track to look over your completed Tracking Sheet and help you double-check to see if anything is incorrect. Not every Actor may be willing to do this, and some may actually give you more information than you need. However, it is worth asking, if it means you get the chance to learn or correct even one item on your Tracking Sheet.

Previews can also be a very nerve-wracking time for the Swings. The stakes are now higher. Just like rehearsals, things are changing every day and there is a chance of being called to go on for a cast member at any time. But now there is an audience and a show that does not stop (hopefully). So, the pressure is on (big time) for the Swings to be on their game. Also, costumes and wigs have been added. This can be tricky onstage and off. Costume/wig changes are another important element of the Track. And, recognizing cast-mates in those new costumes and wigs onstage can also be a challenge.

Oh, and did we mention that the entire Creative Team and usually many Producers are in attendance at most of the Previews? (Again, no pressure!) There is also an emotional element involved when an audience shows up. All performers (even Swings) want most to be out there in front of that audience. Waiting in the Wings and doing your duty can take an emotional toll.

> On my first show it was pretty hard [to go through Previews]. It was exciting to be involved in such a momentous occasion, but come show time I would inevitably feel left out of the proceedings. The onstage Company is rewarded for their hard work with the rush and thrill that comes from the introduction of a live audience to the show. As a Swing, not only do you not get to be onstage receiving that feedback and excitement, you also are left to basically fend for yourself; still learning and processing copious amounts of information and worrying over when you are actually going to have to go on and prove to everyone (the Company, Creative Team, Stage Management) that you do deserve to be there and that the show will never look inferior because of your presence. It can be a pretty daunting and heady time. Over the years (I've been doing this Swing thing for a while now) it has gotten much easier dealing with this inevitable part of the Broadway creative process. This is mainly because of an increased level of confidence in my "Swing abilities" and also because I have learned that in a few months' time, the job will get easier and become the position coveted by more and more of the Company.
>
> JASON SNOW (*The Little Mermaid,
> The Music Man, Hairspray*)

Backstage Tracking

Another task of the Swings during Previews is learning their "backstage choreography." They might have perfectly drafted charts and cards. They might know their onstage Blocking like the back of their hand. But, what happens between the Ensemble scenes, backstage, is an entirely different element.

Hopefully, Stage Management permits (if not encourages) the Swings to watch the show from backstage. This is often called *Backstage Tracking*. It is important for the Swings to watch from the Wings to see exactly how the entrances and exits work, how the Actors load onto set pieces, when and where costume changes take place, and any other intricacies that will keep the show running smoothly and safely.

Swings will spend a lot of time in the Wings during Previews. It is important, when doing Backstage Tracking, to spend an entire show watching each Actor that they cover, individually. That means from half-hour wig call until the last costume change into their post-show robes, the Swings should be documenting everything. And by everything, we mean where they change, whom they walk in front of or behind to get on- and offstage, even when they have time to go to the bathroom (very important!). This may seem like overkill. But, the job of the Swing is to step into the show *seamlessly*. When the best Swings are on, the Regular Playing Company does not notice a difference. That is why this attention to detail is so very important. (Trust us, when there is only one bathroom, those scheduled potty breaks are *important*!)

It is always a good idea for Swings to watch *every* quick change they will be involved in. Even if two Actors have the exact same costume change, chances are those two Actors might perform the quick change in a different way. If a Swing has his or her own way of performing a quick change, this could throw off the **Dresser** who helps the Regular Playing Actor each night. There is sometimes a very choreographed order in which the quick change happens (i.e., put on shirt first; Dresser buttons shirt while Actor changes socks; Dresser prepares shoes while Actor puts on pants; Actor ties shoes while Dresser gets jacket; Actor buttons jacket while Dresser puts on the hat and finally hands Actor the gloves, which are put on as he walks towards his entrance). If Swings do not understand this flow (that has already been perfected and is in the Dresser's nightly routine) they may not make their quick change that night. A Swing can always approach the Wardrobe Supervisor and ask to run a particularly tricky quick change ahead of time. Giving the Swing a couple of tries to get the quick change Choreography just right is always helpful.

And, (for all you Swings-to-be out there), it *must* be cleared with Stage Management when the Swings want to do Backstage Tracking. This is, of course, for safety purposes and is of the utmost importance. In some cases, it may be a long while into Previews before Stage Management allows the Swings in the Wings. Many Swings actually prefer to wait a few days or weeks before tracking, to let the Regular Playing Company figure out exactly what they are doing back there.

It is also recommended (and in many cases required) for the Swings to wear all black or dark clothing in the Wings, just like the Crew. (The audience should not see anyone extra in the Wings while they are enjoying the magic of Broadway!) Often, an Assistant Stage Manager will be working on either side of the stage and will gladly help Swings stay out of harm's way. The first time Swings Track backstage, they may feel as though they are in the way of the Actors and Crew. They may even find that they spend more time watching the Crew and being pushed out of the way, than getting any tracking done. But, as they become more and more familiar with the show, they will learn all of the safe places and times to watch—and those moments to just get the heck out of Dodge!

Another consideration while doing Backstage Tracking is respecting the work of the Actors onstage. Previews are a nerve-wracking time for everyone . . . not just the Swings! The onstage Actors are in need of no distractions while they, too, are trying to give a great performance and remember all the changes being made. It is important to be discreet and respectful, while getting the job done.

> I enjoyed letting the first few shows go by for the cast when I wasn't on. They are just as frustrated with costume changes, set moves, and props. It's nice to let them iron out the problem areas and then you can just ask them what the solutions are when it's over. [Also, when tracking backstage] I take along a tape recorder, and write down the notes later.
>
> JENNIE FORD (*An American in Paris, Evita, All Shook up, Urban Cowboy, Hairspray, The Music Man*)

There is always a whole other show that happens offstage in the Wings, backstage, and in the dressing rooms. There is a real choreography that happens among the other cast members, the

Dressers, and the rest of the Crew. In *Beauty and the Beast* you had to learn when you could actually be onstage to enter or when you had to exit because the wing space at the Palace was so small and you might get run over by a set piece or an Actor in a costume with limited visual acuity.

MARK S. HOEBEE (*Victor/Victoria, Beauty and the Beast, Nick & Nora, Jerome Robbins' Broadway*)

On one show when I was also covering a Principal role, I was told by the Stage Manager to limit the amount of time I spent shadowing in the wings, because the woman playing the role I was covering was distracted by seeing me offstage during performance. From then on, I tried to be a bit more invisible when her scenes were happening onstage.

ANONYMOUS

5

On with the Show

Opening Night

And finally, the big day arrives. It is Opening Night on Broadway! A Broadway Opening is like no other night for a performer. The excitement has been building for weeks. The dressing rooms and hallways backstage look like a flower shop, with all the gifts and well wishes. The red carpet is laid outside the theatre door; the paparazzi are in place to capture the moment. It is finally here!

And where are the Swings? In their dressing room, in their jeans, wondering if they will watch the show from the front or the wings or just spend the show getting ready for the after party.

Opening Night can really be full of mixed emotions for the Swings. Just like the rest of the cast, the Swings have spent weeks, even months, preparing for this big night. They have done so much work and spent many hours on the show (maybe even more than the regular cast). But, in most cases, the Swings will not step on to the stage on Opening Night, nor will they take a bow with the cast. They will be in their position, at the ready, backstage.

Sometimes, Swings are even given tickets to Opening Night, so that they can watch from the House, in an actual seat (instead of standing in the back). While it is a wonderful gesture, this too can be awkward for the Swings—emotionally. It can be a weird feeling, sitting amongst the audience, watching a show that they have spent months working on. Though they are a crucial part of the cast; that experience can also make them feel like outsiders.

The Opening Night Party, another Broadway tradition, can be a hard night for the Swings. Usually held at a swanky restaurant or hotel, it is a time of celebration for the whole Company. But, the Swings can often feel forgotten. When the cameras are flashing and the photographers arranging group photos, the Swings are often overlooked. It is not hard to understand, the paparazzi does not recognize them from the performance that night, because they were not in it. Nonetheless, it is a tough pill to swallow when everyone seems to be getting recognized, except the Swings.

Beyond feeling left out of Opening Night, it is not guaranteed that Swings will perform in publicity events, such as the Tony Awards, the Macy's Thanksgiving Day Parade, or morning talk shows. They might not even be asked to sing on the Original Broadway Cast Album. These decisions can be made for any number of reasons, including artistic choices or financial/time constraints. While it may seem logical, it does not change the fact that this can make Swings feel further alienated from their cast mates.

But, that is the job of the Swing. Swings take on this responsibility knowing that it is not about the public glory or recognition. Swings will get loads of glory, months on into the show when half the cast is out and the show is saved by every Swing playing multiple parts. That is the glory the Swings live for!

Who is on First?

Once the exuberance of the Opening starts to settle down, the real work begins. For the next few weeks, the Creative Team will start to wean themselves away from the theatre, allowing the show to take on its own breath and life. The Company will of course remain focused and the Swings will begin to wonder, "Who will be the first to call out?"

It almost seems like a bit of a competition at first amongst the Regular Playing Company (in fact we have heard of and been in shows that actually have a competition going). No one really wants to be the first one to bite the dust and call out. But, once the dam breaks . . . the Swings get to show their stuff.

Wardrobe

Swings are often asked, "Do you get your own costumes (or do you have to wear someone else's)?" Good question! And the answer is yes . . . and no. According to the Production Contract, all Actors are required to have their own set of undergarments as well as any costume piece that has direct contact with skin. However, some of the larger accoutrements or very expensive dresses may be shared amongst other Actors. All Actors also must have their own wigs. So, depending on the show, a Swing might have costumes for seven or eight tracks, or they might have a more generic looking costume that will fit in, no matter which Track they are in on any given night.

Swing Costumes also present work for the Wardrobe Crew. If a show has multiple quick changes (and many do), the Wardrobe Crew pre-sets all the costume pieces for the regular players. When they find out that a Swing is going on, they must do a "switch-out," pulling all the parts and pieces out for the Actor who is away and replacing them with the Swing's costumes. This can be particularly stressful when an Actor calls out shortly before **Places** is called, or during a show. And, it can take precious time if the Swing costumes are stored far from the stage area.

And speaking of appreciating the hard-working Wardrobe Crew, it is a Broadway tradition that, at the end of each week, Actors tip their Dressers (the Wardrobe Crew who help Actors make their costume changes). The current standard is $10 per week, for an Ensemble member's main Dresser. For Swings, this can sometimes pose a problem, in terms of knowing how much to tip. Maybe they only went on once that week. Or, perhaps, they were on in five different tracks with five different dressers! There are two ways to handle this. One, the Swings can keep a running list of who they were for each week. When they hit around eight shows with a particular Dresser, they can tip them the weekly amount. Or, two, if the Ensemble pools their money together at the end of each week, the Swings can include an amount that corresponds to how many shows they performed that week.

When a show is first opening, the first priority is the Regular Playing Company. So, when it comes to costumes, often the show will open without the Swings' costumes completed. (Note: Swings should have their costumes by eight weeks after the Official

Opening, as per the Production Contract). This can present some tricky . . . and funny . . . situations for the Swings!

In *First Wives Club*, I went on for four shows in the jeans and sneakers I wore to the theatre that evening because I hadn't had a costume fitting at that point . . . as we were just beginning Previews. (Fortunately, it was a contemporary show, so my street clothes could blend in onstage.)

JENIFER FOOTE (*On the Twentieth Century*,
The Mystery of Edwin Drood, *Rock of Ages*,
A Chorus Line, *Dirty Rotten Scoundrels*)

I've had to wear other people's costumes, and sometimes this was fine, if we were the same size. If the person was smaller than me and I had to squeeze myself into their dress, it was not a happy feeling, believe me. Nothing makes you feel like a big fat giant more than that!

LEAH HOROWITZ (*Thoroughly Modern Millie*,
La Cage Aux Folles, *Fiddler on the Roof*, *The Woman in White*)

Once Upon A Mattress . . . did provide me with my most interesting costume experience. My Swing duties there included an unusually wide variety of roles, a fact which was brought home to me when I had to go on for the character "Merton." Now I am 5'7", 115 lbs and, depending on the cut, can fit into a size 4. Tom Alan Robbins was the Actor who usually played the role. He has also played the warthog in *The Lion King*, so you get the idea of the discrepancy in our sizes. Of course, when I had to go on, I wore his costume with no alterations.

ROSEMARY LOAR (*Once Upon a Mattress*,
Sunset Boulevard)

In the *Grease* revival that opened in 1994 with Rosie O'Donnell, I was going on for a character with a particular costume that I had never worn before. It was a fast change getting into it, so I quickly changed and went onstage. It was the scarf on the head that was the problem. It was meant to be worn like it was blowing in the wind à la Marilyn Monroe. I fastened it incorrectly, so instead of blowing back away from my face, it was standing straight up in the air, making me look like a deacon or the Pope! At intermission I went into the Stage Manager's office, and they all had wrapped newspapers around their head to mimic how I looked! They could hardly contain themselves. We had a long laugh about that!! So, I advise Swings to make sure they understand how their costume works!

> PATTI D'BECK (*Applause, Annie Get Your Gun, The Best Little Whorehouse in Texas, A Chorus Line, Grease, My One and Only, The Will Rogers Follies*)

In *Once Upon A Mattress*, I went on as the Jester with the playing Actor's costume, and hadn't had a Put-In with the orchestra . . . so I get out there and realize that my ears were totally covered by the hood piece, and I couldn't hear *one note* that the band was playing. The playing Actor had had months of running [the show], not to mention the entire Tech and Preview period to get used to the sound, but I was at a total loss and panicked! At the intermission, the brilliant Wardrobe Supervisor (Linda Lee—if you read this, I worship you) cut ear holes into this man's costume so that I could actually hear the music for my Second Act number.

> THOM CHRISTOPHER WARREN (*The Lion King, Once Upon a Mattress*)

On *Pirate Queen* I had a matinee where I ended up going on for someone very last minute and it was a track that had a large number of costume changes. I was going to have to wear many of the costumes of the Actor I was on for but this all happened at the fifteen-minute call. I never tried them before the show and we just said a little prayer during every costume change that it would all come close to fitting me. I think the Dresser was much more nervous than I was. The hardest part about the entire Swing costume drama is that I like to have a moment to myself before the show starts, particularly if I am on in a new track. It's nothing more serious than a moment when I can collect my thoughts and focus but all too often when places is called I have found myself standing in my underwear in the middle of the dressing room waiting for costume pieces to be found.

> JEFF WILLIAMS (*The Pirate Queen, Chitty Chitty Bang Bang, The Music Man*)

Going on for the First Time

In a way, the Swings get two Opening Nights. There is the regular Opening Night with all the "hoopla" and then there is the Swings' Opening Night. The Swings' Opening Night is more likely to be a Wednesday matinee. No red carpet, no party . . . just their first chance to make their debut in the show. It is also probably their first time putting on their costumes and makeup, hearing themselves on mic with the orchestra, and being onstage with all the technical elements.

> Going on for the first time . . . it feels like you are performing at gun-point.
>
> SEAN MacLAUGHLIN (*Lestat, The Woman in White*)

> It was absolutely terrifying. I suddenly felt so unprepared, because I had no idea what it felt like to be onstage with the entire cast, with costumes, with lights, with an audience. There is no way to simulate that experience beforehand. I thought I might die, I was so nervous that very first time.
>
> BETSY MORGAN (*High Fidelity, The Little Mermaid*)

> I just try to concentrate on my job at hand. Who I need to be near, what hole I need to fill, what lines I need to say. I am usually really focused when I am on for the first time, so there isn't a lot of joking, but I *do* take solace in the fact that everyone around me knows what they are doing, so if I just keep my feelers open, then I can do my job without anyone onstage noticing that I was even there.
>
> JUSTIN GREER (*Anything Goes, The Mystery of Edwin Drood, Shrek, The Producers*)

The Swings' Opening Night (much like the many nights to follow when they are on) will likely begin with a phone call, text, or email from Stage Management. Hopefully this will happen several hours before the show, but it may be one hour or even a half-hour before. The Swings will rush to the theatre, if they are not already there, to begin hair and makeup. They will also likely have to report to Wardrobe for fittings, as often the Swings' costumes are the last to be completed.

This is when all the hard work from rehearsals starts to pay off. The charts and cards that the Swings spent hours preparing will really come in handy in these final minutes before they rush onstage. While physically preparing for the show, they will also be mentally preparing . . . cramming a bit, to remember where they are going and what they are doing when they get there.

For a Swing's first time on, the Dance Captains or **Stage Managers** will likely call a brief **Put-In Rehearsal**. (Note: there are a couple of different types of Put-In Rehearsals. Some are called earlier in the day and last a few hours, while others happen at hour or half-hour and are very brief.) In a quick Put-in (at half-hour, before the show), the Company will gather onstage and walk through any tricky Blocking or portions that are of safety concern. If partnering is involved, the Swing will work with his/her onstage partners for the evening to make sure that timing is correct and to "feel" the lifts once before they are in front of an audience. Tight vocal harmonies or solo lines may be quickly rehearsed with the Musical Director or scene work might be walked through with other Principals. These are fast-paced, brush up rehearsals. The Swing should be very prepared at this point, knowing exactly what to do. The focus is to make sure that the Swing and the Regular Playing Company mesh well together and there are no questions. (Stage Management usually works to make sure that any tricky set piece moves or issues of safety are worked out before the Swings go on. But, sometimes there is not time and Swings will have to "wing it" and do the best they can.)

The Swings should always be thinking one step ahead of everyone . . . and Put-Ins are no exception. It is a good idea for the Swings to make notes ahead of time of the sequences and transitions they feel they need to run, or set pieces and props they need to work with before they go on the first time. Often in the message from Stage Management, Swings will be asked, "What do you need at the Put-In?" Well-prepared Swings will be able to look at their list and rattle off exactly what they would like to do. It is also a good idea to prioritize this list as time often runs short. Making a "Must-Do" and "If-There's-Time-To-Do" list will ensure that the most important elements are attended to.

Another important note is that there is not always a Put-In for every first time on in a new Track. This is sometimes due to lack of time, if there is not enough advance notice. Or, if the Swing has been on for several other tracks, it may be assumed that a Put-In is not necessary.

Tips from the Pros

Here are some First-Time-On Tips from our Swings:

> After freaking out after making a few mistakes onstage, I realized I couldn't go on expecting myself to be perfect all the time—especially my first time on in a track. I would tell myself that if I messed up, it would be pretty unlikely that the entire audience would be staring at me at that moment. They'd be looking at the star. Only your mom comes to a show and watches you in the Ensemble the entire time!
>
> LEAH HOROWITZ (*Thoroughly Modern Millie*, *La Cage Aux Folles*, *Fiddler on the Roof*, *The Woman in White*)

> Going on the first time for a new track or a track that you're a little unsure of in spots can feel like an out-of-body experience. But it's the best stage training I've had—there's nothing that can prepare you for feeling like you've been shot out of a cannon than . . . well, getting shot out of a cannon. Even with loads of preparation and rehearsal, the first time or two doing a new show can just feel like that, but the longer you've been with the show and the more tracks you've performed in that show, it does get easier. After a while, it's not a big deal anymore.
>
> ALLYSON TURNER (WILKERSON) (*The Look of Love*, *The Boys From Syracuse*, *Guys and Dolls*—National Tour)

> My main concern at first is making sure I know the traffic patterns. I also try to be keenly aware of what the track does that involves other people. If I make a mistake personally, I can forgive myself, but I don't want to mess anyone else up. That is my main concern . . . does this character bring on an important prop for someone else? Do I need to be out of someone's way who's making a quick change? Those are the first things to think about,

everything else comes into play and you go with your instinct and skill to get through everything else.

KURT DOMONEY (*A Chorus Line,*
The Music Man—Arena Stage)

[*Saturday Night*] *Fever* was so good. When you went on before the show they had rehearsals onstage at fifteen-minute call to go over all partnering for Act One. Intermission you would go over Partnering for Act Two. Taking it one act at a time is very helpful and makes it a lot less overwhelming.

RICHIE MASTASCUSA (*White Christmas,*
Saturday Night Fever)

[In *The*] *Radio City* [*Christmas Spectacular*], the opening number was crazy! We all wore these green outfits that looked like football uniforms. . . . You couldn't tell who was who. At one point in the number, we would form two circles and would chaîné between each other, the circles changing places with each other. Well, the girls, knowing where they were going, would just barrel through. So finally I realized that if I yelled "Swing!" as I did this, the hole would miraculously open and I'd make it to the other side without being bowled over.

CALLIE CARTER (*Evita, Elf, Rock of Ages,*
Spamalot, 42nd Street)

Another tip from experienced Swings is to keep a Swing Journal or a stack of sticky notes handy in preparation to go on. Questions will arise and in the flurry of fittings and Put-Ins, not to mention nerves, these questions will be forgotten, until that moment onstage when you really need the answer.

Austin's List

When a Swing goes on for the first time (or really anytime), it can feel like an overload of tasks. To not feel too overwhelmed, it can be helpful to prioritize. Here is "Austin's List of Priorities for Going On."

1   Safety first!—Don't hurt anyone or yourself. If you don't
    feel safe, don't do it. This is your Number One job—not
    hurting anyone. No matter what happens during the show
    if you can walk off the stage and say, "Well, at least I didn't
    kill anyone," you have done your job.

2   Perform—Breathe and try to be in the moment. Make a
    strong acting choice and go for it. This especially comes in
    handy if you forgot (or didn't yet learn) the Choreography.
    Don't stand there blank faced! Pick an appropriate action
    and play it. Live in the world of the play, every moment you
    are on the stage.

3   Choreography—Even if you have no idea what you are
    saying or singing, just keep doing the Choreography!
    Mouth the words (don't tell the Musical Director I told you
    that), concentrate on the lifts with your partner, don't hurt
    anyone and live in the play. Hit those counts and kick that
    leg! (And then work on getting the parts of the Track that
    you missed down for next time!)

4   Sing –You *must* perform all solos and any special duet/trio/
    tight harmony specialties when you are on. But, for your
    first time in a new Track, in the Ensemble numbers, just
    sing something that fits in the chord. (Again, don't tell the
    Musical Directors!) The more times you go on you can
    plunk out the notes, and get those tricky harmonies. Unless
    you have a picky Musical Director (whom you *will not* tell
    about this advice), no one expects you to be perfect. While
    being a super Swing who sings every note perfectly is a
    good goal, it can be just that—a goal. One caveat: if you are
    swinging a heavy vocal show, perhaps where there is little
    to no movement, then the expectation for more precision
    in the vocal parts is, of course, much higher.

5   Relax and celebrate—Congratulate yourself on a job well
    done. There will always be things you could have done
    better, and you will improve! Make a list of these things on
    your way home. Ask your Dance Captain or the person
    who is usually in the Track about anything you weren't clear
    on. But for right now it's important to delight in a post-
    show treat and celebrate!!

6

And the Show Goes On . . . and On . . . and On . . .

Now that the show and the Swing have both had their Opening Nights, the time comes to settle into the regular routine of the eight-show week. This brings about an entirely new set of challenges for Broadway Swings, maintaining their show during their typical work week.

Show Shape

The first quandary is staying in *show shape*. While the Regular Playing Company has the benefit of doing the show every single performance (therefore maintaining stamina and endurance), the Swings are only on one to two times a week or sometimes even one to two times a month in dry spells. Therefore, it becomes the Swings' responsibility to keep in shape. And "in shape" means a whole slew of things. Not only do Swings need to be in good physical shape in order to get through the show, but also they need to maintain all the show elements they are responsible for. For example, Swings that have to hit a solo high note had better be practicing that even on the nights they are off, so that, when they are on, it seems as though they have been doing the eight shows a week like everyone else. This goes for specialty dance movements, dialects, and harmonies as well. They must rehearse twice as hard as the Regular Playing Company because they do not have the opportunity to do it every single night. It should be noted that any specialty technical elements or stunts involving set pieces or rigging should be practiced on a regular basis, as determined by Stage Management.

A THOUGHT FROM LYNDY

One thing that Swings rarely get to do is rehearse with the band/orchestra. Unless someone is out, the Regular Playing Company will participate in the Sitz Probe and all other rehearsals with the orchestra. So, I always liked to utilize the backstage monitors to help me know what I was going to hear when singing with the band. I would often go into an empty dressing room, during the show, and sing along with the show for practice. (It is important to make sure that you are far enough away from the stage/house, so that no one hears you!) If Management allowed, sometimes we would also dance along to the show, while it was in progress, in the lobby. I actually learned quite a bit of *The Little Mermaid*, dancing in the second-floor lobby at the Lunt-Fontanne. There are fantastic mirrors in that space, so we made it our own little studio and enjoyed performing for the concessions and merchandise staff!

Called Rehearsals

While it is important for the Broadway Swings to be self-disciplined and rehearse themselves, the company will also call them into regular, organized rehearsals from time to time. Typically, weekly or bi-weekly rehearsals are actually held for the Understudies. However, these rehearsals may be open to the Swing Company. Sometimes, Swings are required to attend or can even request to attend these rehearsals. **Understudy Rehearsals** are typically held on the stage with certain elements of the set, certain props, work lights, and a rehearsal pianist. While many other elements are missing (costumes, lights, sound, etc.), this can be the closest that Swings or Understudies can get to simulating their onstage performance. These rehearsals can be a crucial aid, especially when months can go by between performances of a specific Track. It is important to note, as well, that a trend in rehearsal patterns is that when the show has first opened and Understudies and Swings are still doing a bit of catch-up work, rehearsals are often twice per week, at the full hourly capacity allowed by Actors' Equity Association. However, as the show settles into its run, and the covers get more comfortable, these rehearsals are sometimes reduced (until Replacements start coming in, and then it is gang busters all over again!). But, our point is that when Swings come into a show later into its run, they should be prepared for perhaps fewer rehearsals than they may prefer. Therefore, they must be even more resourceful and self-disciplined to stay up to speed.

> Every show is different, but the toughest was *Jerome Robbins' Broadway*. We had rehearsal every Tuesday, Thursday, and Friday through the entire run including the closing week of the Broadway Company—no joke. We were constantly putting someone in or running through the third covers. And in the closing week, Jerome was re-ordering the show for the impending tour, so we would rehearse different show line-ups during the day with different casting and then perform it at night.
>
> MARK S. HOEBEE (*Victor/Victoria*, *Beauty and the Beast*,
> *Nick & Nora*, *Jerome Robbins' Broadway*)

> Understudy rehearsals are very helpful and really show you how much you know and don't know! If you can pull off a track on a mostly empty stage with no props, no scenery, and a fraction of the Actors, you are in good shape.
>
> CYNTHIA LEIGH HEIM (*The Music Man*,
> *The Scarlet Pimpernel*, *Evita*—National Tour)

> In no time a Swing will realize that at these rehearsals, the Swing is present mainly for the benefit of the Understudies. Your presence is to facilitate the learning and rehearsing of the Principal tracks. Swings are usually asked and expected to perform multiple tracks in order to keep the Principal parts moving through the show with as much aid as possible.
>
> JASON SNOW (*The Little Mermaid*,
> *The Music Man*, *Hairspray*)

Staying Focused

In addition to staying in good physical and vocal shape, it is essential for Swings to stay in good mental shape. The worst feeling is being five minutes to Places and hearing your name called over the loudspeaker to go on for a Track that you have not reviewed in a long time. For this reason, it is a good idea to stay on top of all your tracks. By consistently going over notes, charts, and cards, as well as tracking backstage and front of House, good Swings have everything fairly fresh in their mind. This way, when that panicky moment of being called on right before or during a show happens (and it *will* happen), it is not nearly as stressful.

> I found myself reviewing my notes a lot during the day. Instead of the newspaper, I would go through the notes of someone's track. The whole experience was a balance of being in control in a situation that could possibly be overwhelming and, at times, chaotic.
>
> KURT DOMONEY (*A Chorus Line,*
> *The Music Man*—Arena Stage)

> I think watching from the house at least once or twice a week is a really good tool and one that if you've been swinging a show for a while is not always easy to do. Another great tool that I used all the time swinging was [tracking] when I was onstage. Once I became comfortable in a few tracks to the point where I didn't have to focus or think as much about where I was going, I began to track while onstage. I could really see the traffic and where people were going up or down stage, left or right, etc., because you are on the stage. That comes later when you really feel at home in a few tracks so you can open up your eyes and do two things at once. Most good Swings I know are multi-taskers!
>
> ALEXIS CARRA (*Wicked, Sweet Charity*)

> I found monitors [in the Stage Manager's booth] that had every view of the stage *extremely* helpful. I never sang along or danced in the wings or anything like that while watching. I have seen people do that . . . it is just distracting to the Actors onstage.
>
> SEAN MacLAUGHLIN (*Lestat, The Woman in White*)

Ch-Ch-Ch-Changes

It is very important for Swings to keep their eye on the show in general. As the show begins to grow into its long run (and the Creative Team's presence wanes), Swings may start to see subtle changes in the show. It is just the natural progression of a long-running show. The beauty of theatre is that it is a live art form with living, breathing, human beings. Thus, the show itself becomes a living organism as well. Just like a person, the show will grow, develop and, *yes*, change—slightly (and sometimes not so slightly). The changes should be minor. The integrity and original conception of the show should stay intact. And it is the responsibility of the Dance Captain, Stage Managers, and Associate Directors and Choreographers to ensure that. However, it is also the responsibility of the Swings to "go with the flow" a bit and not get too stressed when the notes they took in rehearsals and Tech are not as up-to-date anymore. Keep an eraser handy, kids!

Also, sometimes the show and those in it every night do not necessarily even notice the metamorphosis, because they are part of it, creating it, and intimately involved with it every night. Yet the Swings, who may see a certain Track once every couple of months, are starkly aware of the change. "Wait a minute, when we opened, she used to go behind so-and-so to get to **Stage Left**, and now she goes in front," a Swing might say. When Swings are watching the show often, they will notice these slight changes and incorporate them into their notes. If it is something that seems drastic, the Swings might approach the Dance Captain, just to verify that this is a new incorporation into the Track. (Or perhaps, it is that sneaky Actor again, just changing things for fun—in which case they will get a note from the DC and be adjusted back to the old way.) What is *not* ideal in this situation is noticing these little changes while onstage—performing the Track. Often, the realization is less of a calm epiphany and more of a painful or panicked moment, e.g., when you have just plowed into the Leading Lady and you do not know why. The lesson to be learned is to watch the show!

One situation that occurred to me was in *Jerome Robbins' Broadway* during the *West Side Story* suite. I had copious notes about the fight choreography between the Sharks and the Jets. Unbeknownst to me, one couple had altered a move and when I went on for one of the guys and was expecting a punch in the stomach, I got a right cross to my jaw and was almost knocked out. Only afterwards did the guys tell me they had recently decided among themselves to change that.

MARK S. HOEBEE (*Victor/Victoria*, *Beauty and the Beast*, *Nick & Nora*, *Jerome Robbins' Broadway*)

We recommend that Swings watch the show, all the way through, at least once a week. This does not necessarily mean that you have to watch it all in one sitting. In fact, sometimes that can be difficult to do. Watching Act One on one night and Act Two on another is a good way to divide the time and be able to accomplish other tasks during the week.

Swings may also have to find interesting places to watch the show (all of the seats may be taken . . . including standing room). They should make friends with the House Manager and the Ushers, and work out *with* them ideal locations to watch the show. (We suggest writing their names down in a Swing Journal and taking an interest in getting to know some new allies.) The Swings will enjoy being cheered on by these great people, when they finally do make their first appearance on the stage. Depending on the Crew and the theatre's policies, some of the best places to watch the show might be the soundboard, Stage Manager's call desk, or lighting booth. But, always ask first!

Covering for Replacement Actors

Another interesting "go with the flow" moment is when Replacements start coming into the show. No two Actors are alike, and when a new person replaces someone in one of your tracks, things will often change. This can be anything from a structured change that affects the Blocking (i.e., the Replacement is shorter than the original Actor and therefore is put in the front row instead of the back) to a subtle change in traffic patterns or improv moments. Regardless, it is important for the Swings to keep their eyes peeled at all times for these slight changes that should be then recorded in their notes.

Split-Tracks and Cross-Gender Swinging

Swings can be also be presented with other unique challenges, including performing Split-Tracks or swinging cross-gender. A Split-Track happens when more Actors are out of the show than there are Swings in the building to cover them. So, one Swing will actually go on for two people at the same time. How is this possible? Certain elements of the two tracks that are not as necessary to the show are eliminated, resulting in a **Cut-Show**. This allows the Swing to jump back and forth between the two tracks throughout the show. For example, the Swing might start the show in Track A because that person has a solo line in the Opening Scene, then jump to Track B for some featured dance moments in the next two numbers, then back to Track A for a scene involving one of the Principals, then back to Track B for the rest of the show. This is the ultimate mental challenge for the Swings. Not only do they have to have two tracks going in their head at the same time, they have to remember which one they are performing in each scene.

In *Jerome Robbins' Broadway*, almost every time we went on was a Split-Track. This was an extremely hard dance show and there were injuries all the time. We had a physical therapist (the first in a Broadway show) working backstage up until the intermission. This particular time I was on in the *On the Town* section with another Swing (Mark S. Hoebee). We both knew the show very well, and during the course of the number my neck started killing me. I turned to Mark and asked him to switch tracks midway through because the track that I was on for (Joey McKneely) stayed on the entire time and his track (Michael Scott Gregory) had a break in the middle of the dance. He said sure, I raced downstairs to the therapist who worked on my neck and then went back upstairs to rejoin the number when the other performer would have [rejoined].

GREGORY GARRISON (*Beauty and the Beast*,
Jerome Robbins' Broadway, *Me and My Girl*)

A SWING'S LIFE: THE FICTIONAL MUSICAL CUT SHOW Tracking for Sunday Matinee Eric, Mike, Colin and Chuck are OUT - The Swings, Austin and David are ON				
ACT I	Eric	Mike	Colin	Chuck
Got a lot of Swinging to do	Austin	CUT	CUT ***Austin moves table	David
Swing on Over Here	Austin	CUT ***Austin lifts Lisa ***David takes the Line "Why?"	CUT	David
Scene 4	Austin	CUT	CUT *Fred track will move the cart	David
There is nothing like a Swing	Austin	CUT	CUT *Karen will leave the stage for partnering section	David
You're on!	Austin	CUT ***Austin will take the song solo	David	CUT ***David will take Chuck's improv dance moment
ACT II				
Scene 2	**Lyndy	Austin	David	CUT
Swinging on Broadway	**Lyndy - doing all but partnering w/ Lisa (exits after wedge)	Austin	David	CUT
Where do we Swing from here?	Austin	CUT	CUT	David
Finale/Bows	Austin	CUT	CUT	David

*Fred, Lisa & Karen are Regular Playing Ensemble members **Lyndy is the female Swing

FIGURE 4 *Example of a Cut-Show Sheet, illustrating Split-Tracks.*

I often do Split-Tracks, and *love* it when I do. I feel like I am saving the show!!! In *Shrek*, I have quadruple-tracked in a show, and have played nine different tracks in the span of one week.

> JUSTIN GREER (*Anything Goes, The Mystery of Edwin Drood, Shrek, The Producers*)

One night, in *Phantom*, I had to cover two roles in the show at the same time. One role was the confidant with a painted white face and bright pink cheeks, etc. The other role was a Christine Daaé double in the white negligee gown. I had no time to paint my full face to perform the confidant while doing the double track so I just painted half of my face, that was upstage facing, white for the confidant and wore Christine's gown and appeared onstage with only my downstage side of face showing!!! No one ever knew the difference!! Theatre magic!

JANET SAIA (The Phantom of the Opera)

In *A Chorus Line*, we were on so often you had to look down at your costume sometimes to make sure you knew who you were on for that night. Or in *Chicago*, we had so many people off one day that we did "Cell Block Tango" with one empty chair! Flying on adrenaline makes you feel so awesome!

DEONE ZANOTTO (A Chorus Line,
Chicago—Australia and Asia)

I once "triple-tracked" in *Rock of Ages*, playing a Principal and two Ensemble tracks in one show. We were stuffing wigs and hats together to try and make me look like different characters. I was underdressed in three separate costumes at one point. I remember after the curtain call I walked off and fell in a heap and just cried in relief.

JOHN O'HARA (Cats, Rock of Ages—Australia)

Many times in *Saturday Night Fever* we would do Split-Tracks. One time I started the show as an Italian American, then I became Latin and then I finished the show as an African American.

RICHIE MASTASCUSA (White Christmas,
Saturday Night Fever)

Swings may also be asked to go on for a part that someone of the opposite sex covers. All shows handle this differently, as no two shows are alike. From what we have heard from various Swings, these tracks are usually in scenes or numbers that are gender-ambiguous (i.e., everyone is dressed as an animal, or other non-gender-specific character) or a general townsperson scene where an Actor can appear as a man or a woman, though the Track is usually played by someone of a specific gender. In situations like this, it means that Swings might essentially double the amount of tracks covered in a given number—which can be a huge increase in workload! And, sometimes, in rare occasions, we have heard of guys in gals' clothing or vice versa, just to keep the show afloat. Usually when this kind of request is made to a Swing it is in the midst of dire situations when the number of Company members missing is so high, the show is being compromised. It is not a normal occurrence (at least we hope).

I would often have to play Asian characters in *Miss Saigon* (I'm Caucasian), which involved lots of sunglasses, big hats and hair gel. I would also dance women's tracks in a mask. I was usually about a foot taller than the other "girls."

KARL CHRISTIAN (*Miss Saigon*, *Beauty and the Beast*, *Jumpers*)

I have been on for a boy in *The Music Man*. The cross-gender swinging was humiliating and frustrating. The humiliation was because the Wardrobe and Hair departments were unprepared and I ended up going on wearing the boy's clothes and French braiding my hair. I felt like, "This is Broadway?"

JENNIE FORD (*An American in Paris*, *Evita*, *All Shook Up*, *Urban Cowboy*, *Hairspray*, *The Music Man*)

We had two people out—a male in a small Principal role and our only male Swing. There was much shuffling and scrambling to get all the parts covered, but there was one scene where there was a problem. There was a crucial bit of exposition in a short scene in the beginning that had to be covered, but there was no male available to do it. The Director happened to be there that day and there was a major brainstorming session to fix this problem. I had an entire scene to learn in just minutes—Wardrobe found me a pair of dark sunglasses, I got into costume, and the overture started. I made my entrance as a secret "spy" (hence the sunglasses), delivered my lines in the scene, exited the stage—and did a happy dance in the wings. I don't think I've *ever* been under the gun like that to learn something so quickly and go out and do it on a Broadway stage minutes later—in front of a paying audience!

ALLYSON TURNER (WILKERSON) (*The Look of Love*, *The Boys From Syracuse*, *Guys and Dolls*—National Tour)

Being "Thrown On"

Another challenge, during the run of a show, is being "thrown on." This means that there is absolutely no advance notice. The Swings find out either a few minutes before the curtain rises or in the middle of a performance that someone has gotten sick or hurt, and they are on!

When an Actor gets sick or injured mid-show, it is important that Stage Management be able to find the Swings quickly. Since Swings may be in a variety of different places, during a performance, some Production Stage Managers create a "Swing Locator Board." At the beginning of each show, the Swings will post where they plan to be for that particular performance (i.e., watching from the balcony, watching from the sound booth, staying in the dressing room/green room or anywhere else the Swing may venture that day). This helps the Stage Managers to quickly locate a Swing, if someone goes down in the middle of the show. Swings should also *always* have their charged cell phone (on silent) right by their side, in case Stage Management needs to contact them.

I have often been thrown on in the middle of the show. Usually it is because someone is sick or injured. It is stressful because you have no time to look at notes or prepare. You really need to be ready and know your tracks. I never feared however asking for help. Sometimes I would ask other Swings to meet me in the wings with their notes and help coach me through stuff. Or I would seek out a dance partner and warn them of my trepidation about a certain lift or sequence. What you learn is that there is a lot of conversation that happens onstage and backstage that the audience is not aware of. I was never shy to say to a fellow performer—even onstage—"Hey, I am on for _____, am I in the right place?" Most fellow Actors are very helpful.

MARK S. HOEBEE (Victor/Victoria, Beauty and the Beast,
Nick & Nora, Jerome Robbins' Broadway)

I was understudying Zaneeta in The Music Man. I was in the house watching the show when Zaneeta twisted her ankle onstage and I saw her go down. She crawled offstage and I ran to the dressing room. I knew she had a scene coming up so I threw on my understudy clothes, left my hair the way it was, had no mic, grabbed her props, and headed onstage. It was about a minute in total. When I got onstage I stayed close to the other Actors so their mics would pick up my lines. Then after the quick scene I went to hair to get a mic and wig on for the rest of the show. The Stage Manager was shocked that I made it onstage. He thought for sure he would have to pull the curtain down and stop the show.

JENNIE FORD (An American in Paris, Evita, All Shook Up,
Urban Cowboy, Hairspray, The Music Man)

I've been thrown on in the middle of a show, I've been thrown on to do one number and I've been thrown on just to take a bow. It's crazy! I always think that the audience is thinking, "Who's the random black guy?" when I'm thrown on in the middle of a show.

JODY REYNARD (Legally Blonde, Taboo, Fosse)

My Broadway debut was as a cow. No, seriously, I was thrown on in the first week of Previews as Milky White, with no rehearsal except for the half-hour prior to curtain. The costume required me to do the entire show in tabletop position, with stilts on my arms—and the only thing I could see was about a two-foot square of the stage directly beneath me. Before I went on, the Stage Manager said to me: "Here's all I want you to worry about: Don't fall off the stage, and try not to run into anybody!"

KRISTIN CARBONE (Fiddler on the Roof, Into the Woods)

Another thing to consider, in terms of being "thrown on," is that there is no specific rule regarding how late a Regular Playing Actor can arrive at the theatre, before the Swing is put on for that performance.

It is at the discretion of Stage Management. It's wise to check in with the Stage Manager to find out what their normal policy is, in order to be better prepared.

Downtime

Once the Swings have gone on for all their tracks, had a few panic attacks while being thrown on, and feel really comfortable with their show, they can finally settle in for "real life" as a Swing. This is what some consider the best perk, and others cannot stand—*downtime*! Yes, Swings often have lots of downtime. Whether it is the two-hour break between rehearsal and show, the three-hour break on a two-show day, or the show itself, Swings often find themselves with time to kill.

Visit any Swing's dressing room on Broadway and in addition to dance shoes, notes, and costumes, you are also likely to find other fun items, such as magazines, books, DVD players, video games, knitting needles and yarn, yoga mats, music, and, of course, laptop computers or iPads. For some Swings, this is their favorite time of day. They have done their work, or it is their first night not being on in a while and they can settle in for a few episodes of the latest hit TV show or catch up on their emails.

> I usually read or worked out in the dressing room or green room if there was one. I try not to watch DVDs as I feel that is sort of inappropriate at work especially if you have earphones in and there is an emergency. Sometimes I catch up with phone calls, on email, etc. Or try and work on show things like [my] Swing book, etc.
>
> ALEXIS CARRA (*Wicked, Sweet Charity*)

> I am not good at Swing projects. I hate feeling like I'm missing being with the Company of onstage Actors. I usually like to stay close to where they convene when offstage. That is typically the Stage Manager's office in a Broadway house. I might flip through a magazine . . . but basically just like to connect with friends.
>
> JENIFER FOOTE (*On the Twentieth Century,
> The Mystery of Edwin Drood, Rock of Ages,
> A Chorus Line, Dirty Rotten Scoundrels*)

If I'm still learning, I'm watching. If I'm cocky, I hang in my dressing room and watch movies/TV. I also read a lot and do crossword puzzles.

MERWIN FOARD (*Aladdin*, *The Addams Family*,
Sweeney Todd; total of over sixteen Broadway shows)

If you are lucky to have a real green room, congrats. I have always hung in the dressing room . . . I do many, many crafts and projects including knitting, crocheting, I've beaded a lampshade, made wine glass markers, quilted, worked on photo albums and scrapbooks. The one thing I can't do is read a book, not with the show playing over the monitor. I want to know what is going on with the show, even if I am not on because you never know when you'll be called on!

CYNTHIA LEIGH HEIM (*The Music Man*,
The Scarlet Pimpernel, *Evita*—National Tour)

As the show continued to run for many months in the Minskoff Theatre in New York, I got to the point where I needed extra projects to keep me sane when I wasn't performing. To further my songwriting, I commandeered the only room in the whole building that did not have the monitor blaring . . . the garbage room. I brought in my Casio keyboard and typewriter and set up an office, working on arrangements and harmonies and writing business letters. When Jane Bodle joined our cast, at one point she needed a piano to refresh herself on a harmony. She asked where she could go to find a piano and she was sent to the "music" room. You can just imagine the expression of shock on her face when she opened that door and saw me hunkered over my dinky little Casio amidst the room's unique ambiance.

ROSEMARY LOAR (*Once Upon a Mattress*,
Sunset Boulevard)

It's *social* time. Once you have conquered all your tracks. I like to go visit everyone. Hair and Wardrobe are usually the most fun and they usually have snacks in there.

RICHIE MASTASCUSA (*White Christmas*,
Saturday Night Fever)

One thing I don't think I ever did was sleep. I just couldn't physically do it; although I'd seen other Swings do it! Generally, if I hung out in the dressing room, I'd try to have a quiet activity, to be respectful of the fact that my cast mates had a show to do. If I did want to go stretch or sing, I'd find a spot where I could do that and not get in the way or be heard—in Broadway theatres it can be tough to find such a spot! If I was going to "disappear" to one of my secret spaces, I'd make sure Stage Management knew where to find me if needed.

ALLYSON TURNER (WILKERSON)
(*The Look of Love, The Boys From Syracuse,*
Guys and Dolls—National Tour)

The Swings in *Cabaret* were onstage in every performance, as the cast was also the orchestra in that production. So even if we were not on for one of the onstage roles, we had our Swing tracks which we performed nightly . . . we sat in the bandstand in complete view of the audience, in full costume and blocking, and played our instruments for the entire show from start to finish. That is, of course, an unusual situation.

JEFF SIEBERT (*Chitty Chitty Bang Bang,*
Cabaret, Miss Saigon)

It is important to note a couple of pieces of Dressing Room etiquette when dealing with downtime. First and foremost, Swings should *never ever* turn the monitor/PA system in the dressing room down or off. It can be tempting, when they have heard the show for the umpteenth time and are trying to learn lines for an audition the next day. However, if they were to miss a call from the Stage Manager or if the cast missed their Places call, because they did not hear it, the Swing responsible would be in *big* trouble!

Also, if Swings choose to work on an outside project (crafting, etc.) and want to spread out their materials onto another Actor's dressing station, they should be sure to get permission first! It is important for Swings to remember that even though they may be "off" for the night, the Regular Playing Company is still trying to do their show and need their space in order to do so.

The Swing Dressing Room

On most shows the Swings will be mixed in with the rest of the Ensemble in the dressing rooms. This way, the Swings can feel like they are staying social with their fellow cast mates. However, some Stage Managers like to employ a "Swing Dressing Room." This is usually a dressing room for both the male and female Swings that is separate from the other Ensemble members. This can be an amazing experience for the Swings as they can share notes with ease and not be a part of the "drama" that sometimes ensues before or during the show. It is like living in a happy Swing bubble where you do not have to worry about offending someone if, during that particular show, you want to have a movie night. Be sure to ask for a TV monitor. It is a great way to keep an eye on what is going on onstage and can be an easy way to spot check little moments in the show. (However, that would not replace the need to watch the show out front once a week!)

> I try to have Swing dressing rooms on all the shows I do. It's a pain for Wardrobe and you guys have to get dressed in a different location when you are on, but I try to do it because I think it creates a better work environment. Keeping [Swings] happy and comfortable is important to me.
>
> CLIFFORD SCHWARTZ (Stage Manager of over thirteen Broadway shows)

Swings often look at their downtime as a well-deserved break! After a couple of weeks of going on for multiple tracks, Split-Tracks, last-minute call-outs, etc., the stress can really pile up and be just as damaging as the weekly grind, if not more. Many Swings feel, after a taxing week or two, that a few days off are much needed, and a chance to recharge and rejuvenate for more stress that is to come.

Another reason Swings may enjoy the downtime aspect of their job is that their bodies and voices are not taxed as much as those doing the full eight-show week. For some, the idea of working on Broadway and having a built-in physical and vocal break can be more appealing than performing in the Regular Playing Company.

Listen, with all the work that I do being a Swing, I know how much work I have put in to be prepared. Getting to sit around once in a while is like a benefit for all the work.

MARC OKA (*Bells are Ringing, Fosse, Miss Saigon, Shogun*)

When the Swing gets Sick

Because Swings are not on every night they might also feel extra pressure to keep from getting injured or sick. When the Regular Playing Company is dealing with strained muscles and fatigued vocal cords, the show needs a strong team in the Wings that is rested and ready to go.

It can be frustrating though when you are not feeling well and a cast member cannot understand why you are sick because you do not go on every day. You sometimes feel like you are never allowed to be sick or tired too because you might "offend" someone.

MEREDITH AKINS (*Mamma Mia!, Footloose*—Broadway and First National Tour)

I would say my most difficult moment as a Swing is fighting a sickness or injury. You are the support system for when other people are sick or injured, and I find it terribly difficult to be out of the show. It depends on the structure of the show and if there are other people in the building to cover for you if you can't be there, but on *Come Fly Away* it's been extremely difficult because I'm essentially the first and only male cover for the men's Ensemble. There are other guys who could go on for a couple of tracks, but it would be more difficult to get them into the show and would only be done in an extreme emergency if I were unavailable. It's made me put a huge pressure on myself to stay healthy. Of course safety and health come first, but it's still a difficult position to find yourself in.

COLIN BRADBURY (*Come Fly Away, The Book of Mormon*—First National Tour, *A Chorus Line*—First National Tour)

I was the sickest I'd ever been at work on any show when I made my Broadway debut in *Jersey Boys*. I was only swinging the show in New York temporarily and my departure was imminent, so I had to get onstage or I risked missing my chance entirely. Michelle Bosch (Production Stage Manager) called me in at the end of the matinee and asked, "Wanna be on Broadway?" "Yeah," I said, struggling to stand up straight. I got a name of a midtown doctor's office from another Swing, ran straight there from the August Wilson, and looked over show notes while I waited. The doctor came in while I was practicing the numbers. I said, "I've wanted to be on Broadway since I was a kid, I've been sick for ten days, I've had an awful sinus infection for at least thirty-six hours, and I'm making my debut in under two hours." She stuck a needle in my arm, told me to inhale Afrin before the entrances, and then wrote me some prescriptions. I ran to the pharmacy and back to the theatre just in time for half-hour, with no time to stop for dinner. I avoided physical contact, stifled every cough, and sweat straight through every one of my eighteen costumes. My motivation for each scene was to make my exit before vomiting. And it was still one of the most thrilling moments of my life, shared with a spectacularly supportive and talented group of people.

COLIN TRAHAN (*Jersey Boys*—Broadway,
Vegas, National Tour)

On or Off?

Clearly there are just as many pros as there are cons to being on in a show or having a night offstage. The Swings are definitely mixed about which they prefer better.

It depends on the show. During *Charity*, [I wanted to be on] all the time because it was so fun to perform all the different tracks. In *Wicked*, I honestly preferred to not be on . . . maybe two or three times a week.

ALEXIS CARRA (*Wicked, Sweet Charity*)

[I prefer] being on! To be clear, being on in one track for several shows is ideal! Being on all week as a different track every night can literally make you feel crazy and schizophrenic.

BROOKE LEIGH ENGEN (*Gypsy, Hairspray*)

I don't mind not being on, but I am not happy if too much time passes between being on. It is more challenging the longer you have not been on.

CYNTHIA LEIGH HEIM (*The Music Man, The Scarlet Pimpernel, Evita*—National Tour)

It depends on the show and the individual tracks I'm required to cover. The best part of being a Swing is that after the initial few months of intense hard work and pressure to learn and perform your multiple covers, you get the luxury of nights off from the show, as well as a solid understanding of how the show works from many perspectives. It is also harder to get bored as you are given the chance to perform with many different dance and scene partners. Constantly having to change things up helps to keep a Swing fresh over the course of a long run.

JASON SNOW (*The Little Mermaid, The Music Man, Hairspray*)

I'd rather perform than sit any day.

MELANIE VAUGHAN (*Ring of Fire, Imaginary Friends*)

Hopefully, from here Swings settle in for a nice, long successful run on Broadway! Enjoying their nights on, their time off and all the ups and downs in between is all part of the long-run experience for a Swing.

7

Closing Time

Like all good things, Broadway shows do come to an inevitable end. Handling the closing of a show is another interesting journey for the Swing.

If the Company is lucky enough to get advance notice of their closing (more than a couple of weeks), Swings can start to prepare themselves emotionally. They will probably notice that members of the Regular Playing Company are beginning to cancel previously scheduled personal days and vacations, and call out less and less. This may happen for two reasons—money and time. No one wants to lose payment for days off when the paychecks are coming to an end. And everyone wants to soak up every last second of their Broadway experience. Unfortunately, the Swings are hoping to savor these last moments as well, but may not get the opportunity.

Many Swings get frustrated that they never really know when their Closing Night will be. Some will never go on again after the Closing Notice. Others might get a few more shots. But, Swings should savor every one of these post-notice performances, especially since they do not know if it is their last. This can be emotionally exhausting for the Swing.

A THOUGHT FROM LYNDY

I felt like I had eighteen Closing Nights at *A Chorus Line*, complete with tears and the feeling that this was it. And then they would call me the next day to go on again. I never wanted to waste the moment. The hardest moment was in the matinee on the last day of the show. I thought I was going on for the closing performance that night and saved my tears a bit in the matinee. About an hour before the show I found out that I would not go on for closing. I really wish I had let it out in the matinee . . . I never got that moment back.

Closing Week and Closing Night can be just as difficult as Opening. During the Closing Week, the Swings start to clean out their dressing rooms. They have practically moved in with their books, computers, and changes of clothes, so this can be an emotional time. And most likely, they will not be on for Closing Night. Many shows' Producers/ Creative Teams prefer not to change Blocking or unpack costumes to give Swings an extra chance to perform. Sometimes, they will get to come onstage for the final bows. Other times, they may have to grieve the loss of their show from the Wings. Or, perhaps most poignantly, they finish their time in the Broadway theatre where they started—in the House, watching the show.

> I am a big fan of putting the Swings on in the closing show of a production. Whether it's just the bows, or a group scene or something. I think it's important that every cast member gets to experience their closing at whatever level the production will allow.
> JENIFER FOOTE (*On the Twentieth Century,*
> *The Mystery of Edwin Drood, Rock of Ages,*
> *A Chorus Line, Dirty Rotten Scoundrels*)

From there, it is off to the Closing Night party and then . . . back to the grind of unemployment and auditions. Perhaps they will Swing in their next show, perhaps they will not; perhaps it will be Broadway, a National Tour, or a Regional Company. Maybe they will go on to Choreography or directing jobs. (Often Swings and/or Dance Captains are asked to re-set Choreography for tours or future productions of the show.) Who knows?! But, their chapter as a Broadway Swing will be closed (for that show) and they will be on to new adventures.

Once a Swing, Always a Swing?

We asked the Broadway Swings if, after their Swing experiences, they would ever want to do it again.

I always think I wouldn't want to, but here I am again. And I think I'm in a place where it's a good fit for me.

> JENIFER FOOTE (*On the Twentieth Century,*
> *The Mystery of Edwin Drood, Rock of Ages,*
> *A Chorus Line, Dirty Rotten Scoundrels*)

I find, when I'm swinging a show, I can sit with the show longer, because I like variety. Personally, when I'm doing the same thing all the time I get antsy. Swinging mixes things up and I like that. It's great. It's really easy for me and it's fun. However, if you're not on for a while, you don't get that adrenaline rush and you miss the stimulation. I like having to use my brain. I guess, in a way, it's a luxury to go on and just do the same show, but for me it's not as challenging.

> JOANNE MANNING (*The Little Mermaid,*
> *The Wedding Singer, Chitty Chitty Bang Bang,*
> *Frogs, Contact, Victor/Victoria*)

I take every job as it comes.

> MERWIN FOARD (*Aladdin, The Addams Family,*
> *Sweeney Todd*; total of over sixteen Broadway shows)

In this economy . . . Never say Never!!

> CYNTHIA LEIGH HEIM (*The Music Man,*
> *The Scarlet Pimpernel, Evita*—National Tour)

It would depend on the show and I'd wanna be *well* compensated.

> JODY REYNARD (*Legally Blonde, Taboo, Fosse*)

No, I thrive on my daily routine.

> ALLYSON TURNER (Wilkerson) (*The Look of Love,*
> *The Boys From Syracuse, Guys and Dolls*—National Tour)

It was humbling, but I was incredibly proud of what I was able to achieve. Since then, I have been an onstage cast member in other shows. I hope I was generous before, but now, I am incredibly generous to and respectful of the brilliant people that can step into many different roles at a moment's notice.

> TODD BUONOPANE (*The 25th Annual Putnam*
> *County Spelling Bee*)

Not in a million years.

> MELANIE VAUGHAN (*Ring of Fire, Imaginary Friends*)

And, we asked the Creative and Casting Departments their thoughts on this, as well.

When someone has been a Swing and then turns down the opportunity to swing again, it is a personal decision. I do not take it personally or hold it against an Actor. Sometimes those decisions pay off and the Actor begins to do other types of roles and sometimes the Actor just doesn't work right away. It can be a gamble, but it is a personal decision that I respect.

> ERIC WOODALL (Casting Director, Tara Rubin Casting)

I would also expect a Swing to be honest with me and say, "Tara, I loved swinging with you and working with you but I really want to be onstage." Be clear. I can't tell you what you want. I can tell you if you're good at it. I know many Swings who are fantastic at it, [but] don't want to swing. Should they then take it off their resumé? Yeah, they should. If they don't want to swing they can just put Ensemble. [But] if they want to swing [they] should have Swing all over [their] resumé. I think Actors should swing once, if they have the opportunity. I think you learn a lot from it. If you've never done anything like that it doesn't get better than just sitting there and being able to absorb all this information. You don't get that in college.

> TARA YOUNG (Associate Director/
> Choreographer on ten Broadway shows)

A THOUGHT FROM AUSTIN

How to help your Swings, if you are a member of the Regular Playing Company:

1 Ask if they need help—If Swings seem overwhelmed or panicked, check in and see if there's anything you can do to help. Maybe you can answer a last-minute question, review some partnering, or grab some food for them, while they

scramble to get ready. If you get the feeling they want to be left alone, then offering a little space or a silent hug works just as well.

2   Let it go—If you find a Swing is in the wrong place and it's not going to hurt anyone, wait until after the show to tell him or her. Better yet, give the note to Stage Management (if it's a Blocking note) or the Dance Captain (if it relates to Choreography).

3   Shove with love—If you find a Swing is in the wrong place, and will potentially hurt himself or herself (or others), then shove with love! As long as it is done with love and you follow up with them, the "shove" part will be forgiven.

4   Don't expect the same show—Whenever a different person steps into a Track, things like partnering, acting moments, or even little inside jokes with the Regular Playing Actor may be different. Try to remind yourself that we all come in different sizes, shapes, and training backgrounds. Things are simply going to *feel* different or strange, because you are not used to them. When safety is involved, it is important that you feel safe, so request as many rehearsals with a Swing as you need to feel secure. But, with other moments, don't try to force the Swing to do *exactly* what the other Actor does. Try to explore different choices or create new inside jokes with a Swing. You might find something amazing together and have fun in the process.

5   Heads up—Swings love to get a heads up when you know something, like, "My brother is in the hospital, and I'm leaving town tonight." However, don't give them a minute-to-minute progress report about how you may or may not come in tomorrow, i.e., "My throat feels funny. No, it's fine. Wait, do I have a fever? I may or may not be here tomorrow." If you have decided you are going to be out, let them know. Otherwise, the back and forth can drive a Swing absolutely insane.

6   Be mindful of what you say—Put yourself in the shoes of your Swing. It may look like they "have the night off" or get to leave early. But remember, their night can go from reading a magazine to a last-second Split-Track in a matter of minutes. You have the luxury of knowing what you will be doing every single show. Swings think about the show from the moment

they wake up in the morning, when they have to check their phones, to make sure Stage Management hasn't messaged them. Also, try to not show your disappointment if you have guests at the show and a Swing is on: "Ah man, my sister is here and people are out tonight."

7 Include your Swings—Say "hi" to them if you haven't seen them in a while. Look forward to creating new moments onstage with the Swings. And if they make a mistake, show a little mercy and remember they are human too! Congratulate them when they have a triumph. Console them when things didn't go as planned. Other people may not understand how hard their job is, so make sure you throw a "Swing Appreciation Day" every once in a while.

Famous Broadway Swings

Norbert Leo Butz—*Rent*
Barrett Foa—*Mamma Mia!*
Jonathan Groff—*In My Life*
Jeremy Jordan—*Rock of Ages*
John Cameron Mitchell—*Big River*
Donna Murphy—*They're Playing our Song*
Karen Olivo—*Rent*
Orfeh—*Footloose*
Brad Oscar—*Aspects of Love*
Jai Rodriguez—*Rent*
Krysta Rodriguez—*Good Vibrations*
Marla Schaffel—*Les Misérables*
J. Robert Spencer—*Side Show*
Tony Yazbeck—*Oklahoma, Never Gonna Dance*

8

So You Think You Can Swing?

Okay, so you think you can swing? From seasoned professionals, here are some things to think about for all of you who are considering becoming a Swing or are preparing for your first time as a Swing.

Do You Have What it Takes?

Most Swings agree that there are a few common denominators among Swings who find success and joy in what they do:

1 Organization—A knack for organization does help. Or, at least having an organized mind is key. Keeping up with multiple tracks, costume information, and changes within the show definitely requires clear and organized thinking.

> That special brain that allows you to compartmentalize information—it's a truly special skill.
> MERWIN FOARD (*Aladdin*, *The Addams Family*, *Sweeney Todd*; total of over sixteen Broadway shows)

2 Versatility—The more skills you have, the more qualified you will be to swing a Broadway show. Proficiency (or better yet, *beyond* proficiency) in acting, voice, dance, dialects, and partnering should be considered a requirement. Tumbling, skating, playing an instrument, circus skills, or aerial arts are

great extras. The more tricks up your sleeve, the better your chances of landing a job as a Broadway Swing.

> It takes a good memory, the ability to pick up choreography and blocking quickly, the ability to be a good partner (scene and dance), a good ear for harmonies, a good eye to see how traffic moves onstage, a lot of common sense, and a desire to do good work onstage!
>
> JODY REYNARD (*Legally Blonde*, *Taboo*, *Fosse*)

3 Spatial awareness—This may seem like a no-brainer, but sometimes we do not even realize how little we pay attention to those around us. Onstage, Swings cannot just worry about themselves, they have to be thinking about everyone else onstage as well.

> Make yourself as comfortable as you can in each track while making your fellow Actors as comfortable as you can in each track.
>
> SEAN MacLAUGHLIN (*Lestat*, *The Woman in White*)

4 "The fine line"—Swings have to walk a fine line between striving for perfection and being able to forgive themselves. Undoubtedly, you *will* make mistakes onstage as a Swing and the undying perfectionist has to be able to let this go. On the other hand, those who do not pay enough attention to detail may make too many mistakes and be a liability to the show. This is a difficult balance to achieve, but necessary!

> I think good Swings do not beat up on themselves, yet always try actively to correct their mistakes. There are some Swings that do minimal work. They just want to be in the "vicinity" of a spot onstage as opposed to a number. Good Swings do not get "married" to blocking because blocking will change. They are not afraid to ask questions or apologize if there is a big mistake. Good Swings know that their job is hard and the homework they must do makes it harder. And good Swings have fun onstage . . . eventually.
>
> MEREDITH AKINS (*Mamma Mia!*, *Footloose*—
> Broadway and First National Tour)

5   Going with the flow—Things *change*—from Blocking, to whom you cover, to who is out from half-hour to Places. Good Swings must be able to adapt to this change easily . . . and better yet, without too much drama!

> There are many people who are definitely not cut out to be Swings. A Swing has to get excited by the unknown. They have to be thrilled by going on at a moment's notice, doing something brand new. A lot of performers are terrified of this.
> ERIC WOODALL (Casting Director, Tara Rubin Casting)

Honing Your Swing Skills

Here are some thoughts from the Swings on how to practice Swing skills:

> When you're in class, don't stand in the same spot the whole time. Swings need to be able to adapt to different spacing constantly. And take ballet. Doing a dance combination to the opposite side clicks into the part of the brain that Swings use whenever they go on.
> IAN LIBERTO (*Promises Promises, Billy Elliot, How to Succeed . . ., Evita*—National Tour)

> When I teach at George Brown College in Toronto, I make all of my students practice swinging. I choreograph three pieces over the semester, where they are only in two. They must then create a Swing book for the piece they have not been choreographed in, and at the exam, I "swing" them into the piece to see how they do. It's a skill that you end up having to figure out what works for you individually.
> STEPHEN ROBERTS (*Oliver!*—Stratford Shakespeare Festival, *Mary Poppins*—National Tour)

> I think it's all about developing an ability to look both at the bigger picture and at the tiny details. When you're rehearsing a scene or a dance number, don't just think about your own blocking and

choreography. Pay attention to the pictures that the Choreographer and Director are forming, the intention of the scene and the characters in it (including the Ensemble!), when groups are dancing on the same foot or opposite (and learn how to reverse things quickly and easily), intricacies of the style, etc. And finally, devise a system for writing down blocking and choreography that works for you. It should be detailed enough to give you any information you might need (where you go onstage, who you partner with, what props you have, etc.), but still be succinct enough to be able to take a quick glance and get the information you need.

ZAK EDWARDS (*Young Frankenstein*—First National Tour)

Honest to God, I would suggest reading *The Four Agreements* by Don Miguel Ruiz: "Don't Take Anything Personally, Don't Make Assumptions, Always Do Your Best, and Be Impeccable with Your Word."

ELIZABETH EARLEY (*Something Rotten, Whistle Down the Wind*—National Tour, *Mary Poppins*—First and Second National Tour)

Start taking meticulous notes of what you do in a show—choreography, direction, entrances, exits, costume changes, props. Everything. Approach each show, when you're not a Swing, like you're swinging just that one track. Use all your rehearsal time wisely both on your feet and in your notes.

LISA KASSAY (*Mary Poppins*—First National Tour, *Hairspray*—First National Tour, *Cats*—National Tour)

I used to learn and sing all the vocal parts in the Choir. Little did I know that my brain was already trained to memorize and handle numerous vocal parts for each track.

JAMAAL WILSON (*The Book of Mormon*—First National Tour)

Learn all forms of vocal styling from opera, classical, pop, 40's, 50's, 60's. Absorb as much dance training/styling as you can from ethnic to ballet to tap. Become a great Actor! Then add in a positive can-do attitude with the desire to make the show the star.

JANET SAIA (*The Phantom of the Opera*)

Tips from the Pros

So, you think you have got the qualifications and honed your skills? You make it through the grueling audition process and actually land a Swing job on Broadway. Are you ready to take on the challenge? Here is some of our best advice, as well as some from a few of our Broadway Swings!

1. Come Prepared

Stock up on all your supplies *before* the first day of rehearsals. Some companies may reimburse you for these supplies. Others may not. Regardless, it is your responsibility to gather everything for yourself.

Supply List:

- Pencils
- *Big* erasers
- Highlighters of various colors
- Notepad (for rehearsal charts and notes)
- Notebook (your Swing Journal)
- Post-it notes of various sizes
- Post-it flags (use different colors to mark important scenes or songs)
- Dividers or divider tabs (to label each scene in your bible)
- Ruler
- Graph paper (can be helpful for rehearsal charts)
- Digital voice recorder
- Index cards (many people prefer the kind that are already spiral bound)
- *Big* three-ring binder (to hold script, score, charts, Tracking Sheets—this will become *your* Show Bible)

- Clipboard
- Back up charger for your phone
- Light-up pen or book light or flashlight app
- Black clothing for Backstage Tracking
- A bag or box that holds your supplies

A THOUGHT FROM AUSTIN

While working on *Little Mermaid*, I had to have a little makeup kit that I could carry to the person's dressing station whenever someone was out. Ever since *Mermaid* I have employed a Swing bag (I use a zipper bank bag) that has all the supplies I need (mic tape, pencil, highlighter, make up, wig prep, hair clips, make up remover pads, mic tape remover, rubbing alcohol pads, Aspirin, band aids, energy bar, almonds, comb, and gum). That way, if I'm thrown on all I have to do is grab my bag, Tracking Sheet and my cell phone, and I'm off. Plus, when you are working in a Broadway house, and your dressing room is on the sixth floor but the Ensemble dressing area is in the basement, you know the hardship of leaving something upstairs in your dressing room . . . it's the worst. This way there is less chance of that happening.

---

2. *Your Swing Journal*

Swings may do this differently, based on personal preference, but it is a good idea to have a separate place (aside from your big binder) to keep miscellaneous bits of info, beginning with the first day of rehearsal. This can be a place to keep your cheat sheet of cast photos (see number 8 in this section), tidbits of news that get tossed out to you as you are walking to the elevator on your way to lunch (like tomorrow someone has a fitting from 3:15 to 4:15 and you will be on), or reminders and notes to yourself. It becomes even more important when you move into the theatre. You can take it with you *everywhere* for those moments when someone will say, "Oh hey, did you know we changed such and such?" Or, "Hey, did Stage Management tell you I am going to be out of town in May, for two weeks?" Or, "Hey, when you were on the other day you handed me that prop wrong." It can also be a great place to take notes when watching the show each week.

3. *Be on Your Feet*

Yes, you do need to be notating what is being taught, but the best way to learn (especially Choreography) is on your feet. Learn to find the balance between physically doing things and writing them down. For every person, it is different. But, you *must* do both.

If you are in a show with a lot of partnering it is a good idea to not only practice it with your fellow Swings, but also seek out people in the cast, with whom you have a relationship, and ask them if they might be willing to come in early or stay late to run some partnering with you.

> It's also a time to start to pick out who you should watch first (as in, if there is an onstage Dance Captain, learn their track first because they will need to swing out, etc.). Sometimes you can get a clue as to who is going to be out a lot within the first week of rehearsals! If so, watch them!
>
> ALEXIS CARRA (*Wicked, Sweet Charity*)

> In music rehearsal I sing along as things are being taught and then try not to be offended if the Musical Director tells the Swings to stop singing so he/she can hear balances, etc.
>
> JEFF WILLIAMS (*The Pirate Queen, Chitty Chitty Bang Bang, The Music Man*)

4. *Do not Distract*

This is one of the humbling elements of the Swing job. During rehearsals, it is not about you. Yes, you must absorb and retain everything that is happening. But, be sure to stay out of the way in run-throughs and any time that the Choreographer or Director really needs to focus on the Regular Playing Company only. Swallow that pride and know that your special days are coming. You are going to save the show one day!

One of the hardest parts about learning a new show as a Swing, is that it's very difficult to find your voice in the room. I sometimes feel like a silent presence in the room . . . observing rather than being able to participate. It can be challenging to not feel like the Creative Team gets to see you first hand doing what you do (your talent).

JENIFER FOOTE (*On the Twentieth Century,*
The Mystery of Edwin Drood, Rock of Ages,
A Chorus Line, Dirty Rotten Scoundrels)

5. *Learning Tracks*

It can be *really* overwhelming to watch a stage of thirty Actors, knowing you have to know what about half of them are doing at all times. Take a deep breath. There are a few different ways to go about this. Think about how you learn best and follow suit. Some people have an easy time seeing whole formations and understanding where each Actor fits into the picture. Others may find it easier to focus on one Track at a time. Whether you are a "big picture" or "one-track-at-a-time" Swing, it does not matter. Do what is best for *you*!

It's totally overwhelming at first. When I describe swinging to new Swings, I love drawing the comparison to a "Magic Eye" picture. The first time I'm up onstage everything looks a bit crazy and disorienting, but if I stare at it long enough, eventually the picture will become clear, and I'll know where to go next . . . hopefully.

BETSY MORGAN (*High Fidelity, The Little Mermaid*)

6. *Be prepared for* Anything

Your first time on might not be after Opening. It might be on the first day of rehearsal. Many things will pull the Regular Playing Company out of the rehearsal room (illness, injury, costume fittings, music rehearsals, coachings). And you, the Swing, will be expected to jump in so business remains as usual. Make sure you have a good enough idea of what all your tracks are doing so that you will be prepared when this time comes.

I will always remember the Assistant Choreographer [of *Damn Yankees*], Kathleen Marshall. She always made me feel that I was a part of the Company. When someone had a costume fitting or was out and there was a dancer missing she would always say "Mark, get up and fill in." This way I could practice with the others.

MARK SANTORO (*Damn Yankees, Cats*)

7. Remember that Replacement Swings are Different

As we mentioned in Chapter 3, if you are a Replacement Swing, your process will be different. Most likely, you will be taught one Track at a time and the rehearsals will actually be focused on you! The drawback is that you will have less time to absorb the show. So, be on your game! Watch every performance, use the stage when you are allowed, and do not waste a minute of time or opportunity to prepare yourself.

In most cases, when taking over for another cover, you aren't given the liberties of finding your own path or journey within the workplace. You follow the same traffic patterns as your predecessor; you will often be expected to replicate that person's habits and idiosyncrasies. It can be difficult to maintain your own identity when stepping into any workplace where you are replacing someone else . . . whether you're taking over for a Swing, a Principal, or a member of the Ensemble.

THOM CHRISTOPHER WARREN (*The Lion King, Once Upon a Mattress*)

As a Replacement Swing, I find it nerve-wracking because I feel like the Dance Captain (or whoever's teaching) always wants me to pick up the show faster than I want or am able to. Either way, a lot of tracks have to be learned quickly and that's daunting!

JODY REYNARD (*Legally Blonde, Taboo, Fosse*)

On *The Pirate Queen* and *Chitty Chitty Bang Bang*, I never even met the Director of either show as they had fled the city by the time I was hired (and I was hired shortly before Opening Night on *Pirate Queen* and about a month after Opening on *Chitty*.) Also, in *Pirate Queen*, there was a good amount of sword fighting and I missed out on all the instruction and training that the rest of the cast got. Instead I had a quick fifteen minutes of "here's the basics" with the fight captain and then proceeded to learn all the fight choreography.

> JEFF WILLIAMS (*The Pirate Queen, Chitty Chitty Bang Bang, The Music Man*)

If you are replacing, ask that person everything you can—Who have they been on for the most? Who has been out the least? Is there anything deceptively tricky about a particular track onstage or off? Would they be willing to share their notes? (If they are, you *must* go over them yourself to see if they are correct.)

> SEAN McKNIGHT (*Anything Goes*—National Tour, *A Christmas Story*—National Tour, *Shrek*—First National Tour)

8. *Names are* Key

On the front of your script, create a color-coded names key that you can also use in your music and notation charts. Keep the colors consistent throughout and it will make life much easier. Also, a key of names to colors is only helpful if you can put a face to a name. Try to learn everyone's name as quickly as possible. This may seem trivial but when you are trying to write your charts and staring at an Actor's face with no recollection of his or her name, it can be very frustrating. Sometimes Stage Management will provide a headshot sheet, with mini-images of everyone's headshots along with their names. This can be a very helpful tool. Request one if it is not given to you. Another option is to Google Image Search your cast mates and create your own document. If you are a Replacement Swing, you can use the headshot page in the Playbill. Using any one of these methods, you can have a quick and easy reference page to place in your notebook.

When making your key and charts, use initials or your own abbreviations (such as F1, M1; Female 1, Male 1, etc.) to help you.

For instance, John Smith would be abbreviated in charts as "JS" and all his text and vocal solos in the script/score would be highlighted green. This is helpful when you have a lot of Tracks that have lines and solos.

Another good idea, related to knowing your cast, is to make sure you put everyone's phone number and email address in your phone. (Stage Management will provide a Contact Sheet with all of this information.) That way, you can contact someone if you need information quickly. Also, this information will come in handy when you receive a text message at half-hour saying, "Hey! So sorry I'm not going to make it today. Calling Stage Management now." If that person is not a contact in your phone, you will waste precious moments trying to figure out who you are on for!

9. Request Set Diagram/Stage Charts

Be sure to request these from Stage Management, especially if you plan to chart out lots of full-stage formations. It is much easier to do this on the diagram than on a blank page. The Stage Manager can usually make lots of copies so you can use them for notation during rehearsal. (See Notation "How-To's" section, in this chapter.)

10. Use Your Breaks

Because the Swings do not get a lot of floor time in rehearsal, use the breaks to get into the space and move. While the Regular Playing Company takes a rest, get onto the floor, move from number to number, and go through the Choreography. Grab a fellow Swing and practice playing various tracks at the same time to start getting a sense of traffic. Sometimes the rest of the Actors will not take a break either, and this can be a good time to ask them to go over things with you. Just remember that this is technically a break for everyone. So if someone is resting, let them rest. Once the show is up and running, find out when you can use the stage to review Choreography or partnering, either before half-hour or during dinner break.

A THOUGHT FROM LYNDY

A great idea, especially for Replacement Swings, is to use the time between shows, on a two-show day, to rehearse on stage. This, of course, requires permission from Stage Management! I used to do this on *The Little Mermaid*. It was really quiet, with no one around, and I had the amazing luxury to walk through all my tracks, get a feel for the space, and practice in my "Mer-Blades." It was so very helpful.

---

11. *Make Friends*

Yes, job number one is getting your work done. But, do take time to socialize . . . especially with the Regular Playing Company. It can be easy to feel left out as a Swing. So, start building the bonds of friendship early, and not just with your fellow Swings. It is also important to befriend your Stage Managers, Dressers, Wardrobe heads, Musical Directors, and Rehearsal Accompanists. Beyond the golden rule of being nice to *everyone*, these are the people who can help you out when push comes to shove. It is always nice to have a good relationship with them, so that when you need favors before a first time on, they will hopefully help you.

Stage Managers and Dance Captains are *really* good friends to have. They can be so helpful in that they too are taking notes on everything that is being set and are a very good resource. When you have questions, this is a good place to start. If they do not have the answers, they will know where to find them.

I think it is important to bond with your fellow Swings as they are the only ones who truly understand what your experience on the show is like. The other Swings are the ones you can [complain] to about the people who are not necessarily Swing-friendly onstage. They are also the people you will spend the most time with during rehearsals, Tech, performances, and Understudy Rehearsals. We had particularly close Swing teams on *A Christmas Carol* and it was always frustrating and disappointing if you felt one member of the team was letting the others down by not doing their job as well as they could. In almost every show I have done, the Swings will watch another Swing when they are on for the first time in a new track and it's great to know you have that support.

JEFF WILLIAMS (*The Pirate Queen,
Chitty Chitty Bang Bang, The Music Man*)

[The ideal backstage relationship is one] where everyone values each other. Swings are a specialty, not a separate entity. I don't like A cast versus B cast talk. . . . If everyone *values* each other and *supports* one another, you can have an awesome show and work environment!

BROOKE LEIGH ENGEN (*Gypsy, Hairspray*)

It's ideal to have a symbiotic relationship: one whose filter is the Dance Captain when there are concerns. But beyond what the work is, then it's just people . . . and people and personalities will either jive, or won't.

ALEXIS CARRA *(Wicked, Sweet Charity)*

12. *Get to Know Your Production Stage Manager (PSM)—and His or Her Routines*

PSMs run their ships differently, with different styles. You need to quickly pick up on how they communicate with you, what they expect, and their protocol. Some things to particularly ask about might be their policies on multiple vacations in one week, swing-outs (planned times when Swings go on for practice), whether or not Swings are allowed to leave earlier than the final curtain, and the cut-off for late arriving Regular Playing Company Actors before putting a Swing on. The better your relationship with your PSM, the better your life in a long-running show will be.

The Stage Managers are your allies as a Swing and I have always tried to cultivate a good relationship with them where I can ask questions, express concerns about particular issues, etc. I have also never been someone who goes to Stage Management to [complain] about things or treated them in some sort of confrontational way. As a result they have always been great to me when I have been on and made sure that I was safe whenever I was backstage.

JEFF WILLIAMS (*The Pirate Queen, Chitty Chitty Bang Bang, The Music Man*)

I think Stage Management can seem scary and is sometimes misconstrued, but they are there to help us, so I try and go to them if I need to. Really, if you are professional and courteous then you are probably going to [get] what you need from them.

ALEXIS CARRA (*Wicked, Sweet Charity*)

I always felt that Stage Management were closer to us Swings than to the rest of the cast. Our jobs often intersected in the way we watched out for patterns of which people were often out, how we worked out vacations, etc. . . . I remember that the Stage Managers always seemed to be grateful to us Swings. They, of all people, recognized how valuable we were to the show.

LYDIA GASTON (*Shogun, Miss Saigon, The King and I*)

I find that if you prove to be a useful and trustworthy Swing early in the run, they will only reward you with respect and constant courtesy. It also helps to always be honest with them and let them know what you need to do your job well. They are managing many people and aspects of the production and aren't always aware of everything you have been given access to or practiced in preparation for performance. Most will accommodate your needs if you communicate [with] them directly and effectively.

JASON SNOW (*The Little Mermaid, The Music Man, Hairspray*)

I like to spend a little bit of extra time checking in on the Swings. I like to think I treat everybody the same. However, I like to give the Swings a little more leeway where I can, in terms of lateness and disciplinary stuff, because there are more times than not that I'll come to them at fifteen [minutes] till show time and ask them to jump through a hoop, or maybe do this move that they're not 100 percent sure of. I like to make an effort to include them in everything. Sometimes they get left out of things, press events that pay extra. This happens especially early on when a show is opening. I like to be a spokesman for Swings. I'm sensitive to people and their job and I think swinging is a little more than "nine to five." You are part of the cast in my eyes, but sometimes not in everyone else's eyes. And that is difficult.

CLIFFORD SCHWARTZ (Stage Manager
of over thirteen Broadway shows)

13. Read the Call Board!

This is not just a place to sign in for rehearsal and turn in your House seat requests. Important information is always up there and it is not always so obvious. Check the costume fitting list, not just for your name but for those you cover. If they are out for a fitting, you will be in their place. Check the **In-Out Sheet** to see if anyone is missing even a portion of rehearsal, because you will have to jump in. Start learning to scan the sign-in sheet. About five minutes before rehearsal starts, casually make your way over to see who has not signed in yet. People will be late or absent, and the sooner you know the better. Do not wait for Stage Management to tell you, be ahead of the game. This habit will come in handy later. When you walk into the theatre for a performance and sign in, check the rest of the sheet. Note who tends to arrive early or late, this will help you give yourself a heads up of when you might be on.

14. *Learn How to Make Mistakes*

It is inevitable. You will make mistakes. You must learn to not *show* the mistake. Recover from it and let it go (both during and after the show). And then learn from the experience in the hope that you never make the same mistake again.

There is a real danger in focusing on mistakes during the performance. If you do this, you run the risk of starting a mistake spiral. While thinking about the mistake that happened in the last scene, you are not allowing yourself to be present in the current scene—therefore becoming susceptible to making more mistakes.

Forgive yourself. Stay in the moment. Swallow your pride and apologize to any parties involved (even though they may not always be as understanding as you would like them to be). You are human and no one should expect you to be perfect all the time. Just try to be better the next time.

As a Swing you are going to make mistakes. You have umpteen tracks in your head and blunders are to be expected. Don't broadcast them by asking people if they saw you mess up. This does you no good. Instead, earmark the error in your brain and go on with your show. When the performer returns to his/her track be sure to watch from the Wings to see how to correct anything that tripped you up.

SEAN McKNIGHT (Anything Goes—National Tour,
A Christmas Story—National Tour, Shrek—First
National Tour)

The show: *The Producers*. The number: "The King of Broadway." The pressure: dancing with Nathan Lane with Susan Stroman in the audience, Warren Carlyle (Stro's associate) sitting next to her and it's one of my first times on as a Swing. Towards the end of the number, the cast forms two lines horizontally across the stage. The next bit of choreography involved the upstage line crossing downstage under the arms of the downstage line. That action repeated several times. Imagine me in my nun's costume—full habit—holding Nathan Lane's hand and dancing downstage with him. We are about to cross under the arms of the downstage line. I have a "hole" to go through and he has a separate "hole" to go through. Well, in my nervous state, I went through Nathan's "hole" with him. This led to the flap of fabric that hangs loosely on a nun's habit getting flipped up over my head causing me to be blinded by black fabric for the next several bars of music. I flailed wildly through the end of the number despite my efforts to regain the choreography and some composure. All I could think of was that I would surely be fired for ruining Stroman's choreography and Nathan's performance. As it turns out, they were all laughing about it and I had five more years as a Swing with the show.

COURTNEY YOUNG (Young Frankenstein,
The Producers, The Full Monty, Little Me)

15. Review and Practice Dangerous or Specialty Skills

As we have mentioned, many shows will include stunts, stage combat, or dangerous specialty skills (e.g., *Spider-Man: Turn off the Dark*, *Starlight Express*). It is your job as a Swing to make sure you stay fresh on these skills. This might mean talking to a Physical Therapist or a Trainer about work-outs that will keep you in shape for these moments in the show. You may not be able to rehearse these moments as often as you would like. And, sometimes Swings might be tempted to say, "I know what that is. I've done it a lot of times." But, remember, it may be months before you go on in that Track again. Like an athlete, you must keep training so that you can go on in a moment's notice.

> [In] *Billy*, I swung four Principals and eight dancers and, in the two weeks of Previews that it played, I went on for four different people. Some of the stuff was so dangerous. All I hoped for was, "Please don't let me hurt anybody." Because in one sequence, when you'd get your guns, they were tossed [to you]—and we were a bunch of dancers. When you went up this rope ladder (and we went up sixty feet in the air) you had to lean out and grab one single rope and they'd let you down. We all had to learn to do that. And we did a pike dance with big huge pikes with pointed ends. I mean it was maddening.
>
> TONY STEVENS (Director/Choreographer of
> Four Broadway shows; Swing on *Billy*)

My Broadway debut was in *Jane Eyre*, as the Swing. That show had two large turntables in concentric circles. Like a bigger donut within a smaller donut that framed a large circle which was the show's main playing space. Sometimes they would spin the same way, sometimes in opposition, and the art of learning to pace your stride so that you could step on to this moving target without being jerked around was tricky to learn and required real-time stage access, which often is sorely lacking for Swings and Understudies, especially in the early stages of a run. So the very first time I was on was for the butler (whose very first entrance involved traversing these giant wheels of spinning death with a full bottle of wine and a wine glass on a tray.) So, of course, I stepped on to the first turntable and my stride was too slow, my body jerked and a full bottle of wine spilled all over the stage. A slightly less than kind member of the Company came over to the spot of my hot-faced shame with a towel and whispered disgustedly "Just get off the stage!" and proceeded to clean up my mess, as I slumped away. This was my first twenty seconds on a Broadway stage.

BRADLEY DEAN (*Jane Eyre*)

16. *Embrace Technology*

Technology can really be helpful for Swings. If you are working on a show that uses Stage Write, you can digitally share your charts with your fellow Swings, Dance Captains, and Assistants. Or, you can use other advances, like Google Drive, Drop Box, or the Cloud, to do your job more efficiently.

One of the greatest helps this past time swinging was using the simple Pages program on Macs and putting all of the information in the Cloud. That way I can access my notes on my computer, iPad, or iPhone. I can alter notes wherever I am and can take my notes with me on my phone. That has been the most helpful for me. Also, stage charts can be scanned into your computer and taken with you wherever.

NATHAN PECK (*Kinky Boots, Dance of the Vampires, Wicked*—Chicago Company)

I still believe that in the first stages of rehearsal the pencil and eraser are your best friends because formations change, scenes get cut, etc. I have fallen in love with the Stage Write app on my iPad. It is an investment, but I have never heard anyone say they didn't like using it. Stage Write allows me to quickly transition from messy pencil charts to clear, color-coded, to-scale drawings; to have my entire show in the palm of my hand, and share charts with fellow Swings. Also, if the Assistant Choreographer is using Stage Write then you can sync up your charts with the Creative Team. It's amazing!

SARA EDWARDS (Associate/Assistant on two Broadway shows; Swing on *Follies*)

I created a set of index cards for each track that I saved as 4 x 6 PDFs in my phone so I could carry it around and reference it whenever needed.

SAM STRASFELD (*An American in Paris,*
Mary Poppins—First National Tour)

17. *Some General Advice*

I have met so many people who have been offered a Swing role whose souls are devastated. It feels like they can't see the forest for the trees. See it as this (if you can) . . . [if] you have been given the opportunity to perfect four or more roles, the production believes you are the person they can rely on and can be great at all of these roles. You will get to go on, and most likely your friends and family will see you—they have to be patient too—like you. Know this is an honor and you will be great.

NICOLA HUMPHREY (*Cats*—Germany/Australia/
New Zealand, *Sesame Street Live*—UK)

Prepare yourself by mastering your workloads. You can expect very little personal help and direction, and very little praise when your name is called. Don't let this affect you. Use this experience as a learning tool. You will learn so much more than you ever could in a class or in college. You will learn humility and you will gain outstanding amounts of quiet confidence in yourself. The opening night lights will never be as bright as they are during your first unscheduled Swing appearance. Become your own Director, and run your own rehearsals. Don't ever complain. And don't let anyone ever hear you complain. Use being a Swing as a learning experience. You are the most valuable and also most expendable member of the cast. Keep a calm demeanor at all times. Everyone knows you will be afraid. If you show it, you will make everyone around you nervous. If you want help from the people who aren't thrilled to be forced into working with someone they haven't rehearsed [with], keep calm, and stay professional. Mistakes are bound to happen. It is inevitable. Prepare yourself as best that you possibly can and then just enjoy your time onstage.

PRESTON ELLIS (*Grease*—First National Tour)

A big thing to tell a Swing early on is, "Don't take anything personally in the next five weeks of this production." And that's really, really important, because when we're working really quickly you can't take it personally. When something is being created [we're] often working with the onstage Actors to create it. If the Swing is following [us] around, as they should, what if they try some sort of lift and the Swing is a little too close? Someone might say, "Listen, just back away for a second." Some people could take that personally, but you can't as a Swing.

TARA YOUNG (Associate Director/
Choreographer on ten Broadway shows)

Let the cast see you at work. Be in the Wings, do the choreography backstage, practice in an on-site studio, watch from the front—anything that keeps you from constantly sitting in the dressing room watching movies, reading books, or talking on your phone. Just don't let anybody see you sleeping on the Equity cot during the show. They won't remember that you just did a triple Split-Track, instead they will view your behavior as complacent and will be unforgiving of any mistake you make. You're an Actor. If you can't bear to be busy, act busy.

SEAN McKNIGHT (*Anything Goes*—National Tour, *A Christmas Story*—National Tour, *Shrek*—First National Tour)

I would say be open enough to understand what everybody is doing and why they're doing it. Don't look at exactly what they're doing. Your job is to find out why they're doing that.

JACK LEE (Musical Director of
nine Broadway shows)

Don't be afraid to get mentored. The first time I was hired as a Swing, my counterpart had swung for *Lion King*, my Dance Captain had swung *Hairspray*, and my Stage Manager had [been a] Dance Captain many times throughout her career. Also, almost ten of the Ensemble members had swung before. I was in great hands to say the least!

STEPHEN ROBERTS (*Oliver!*—Stratford Shakespeare Festival,
Mary Poppins—National Tour)

Notation "How-To's"

We have mentioned before that there are numerous ways to notate all the information for your tracks. Charts, Notecards, and Tracking Sheets are the most popular. (See Chapter 3 for a refresher if you need one.) Now we will go into more detail on exactly *how* to create these documents.

Charts

Rehearsal Charts

These are charts that are created very quickly during rehearsal. They are short-hand, if you will, and always done in pencil. They can be made on a legal pad, in your Swing notebook, or in your script. These charts are the Swings' first attempt at capturing the big picture of each number. They do not need to be fancy, just legible enough, so that if you are thrown into a number in rehearsal you can check to see where you are going. Rehearsal charts will be the basis of the final charts (done by hand or computer).

The most common way to create a rehearsal chart is by using Xs for boys and Os for girls, and/or using initials. (Be sure you create a key beforehand, so you do not waste time trying to remember which initials you are using for whom.) It is a smart idea to always mark which way is **Downstage**. (Sometimes you may chart differently, depending on where you are watching in the room.) Start by putting a zero with a line through it to denote Downstage center (see Figure 5). Create the number line (Stage Numbers) across the top or bottom of the page for reference. Then start creating formations, using the number line as your guide. Be sure to number or name your charts as you go. If you can fit four or five charts on the same page, it will be easier to reference if you have to pop in for someone. Be sure to chart traffic patterns as well, by using arrows. You should not only document formations, but also who passes between whom to get there.

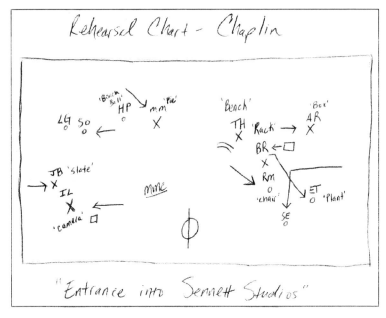

FIGURE 5 *Example of a rehearsal chart.*

Final Charts

After completing rehearsal charts, you can then decide how you want to "finalize" your charts over the next few months. We do not recommend spending too much time on your final charts too early. (You never know when that dance number will be cut or completely restaged a week before opening.) It is a pretty terrible feeling to throw away something that you spent hours on and will potentially never use. On the other hand, do not throw anything away until the show is frozen. (You never know when the Creative Team may say, "You know what, let's go back to the old staging.")

If you are artistically inclined, you might opt for the old-fashioned way of charting by hand—using stage diagrams provided by Stage Management and drawing formations, using initials, names, or colors. Keep things nice and neat by using a ruler to draw straight lines and set pieces. Or, create your charts on a computer. Thanks to the new iPad app "Stage Write," Swings now have a powerful tool for chart making. (See Text Box for more information.) Before the days of Stage Write, programs like Microsoft Word, Publisher, or Photoshop could be used to upload stage diagrams onto a computer to create charts.

Regardless of what medium you use, here are the things that every chart should have:

- A clear Downstage center marker, and number line/Stage Numbers.

- A title indicating the name of the number and the formation depicted. Example: "Opening number—The Wedge" or "Opening Number—Out of the Wedge".

- Page numbers (in case they fall out or get taken out).

- Any intricate Choreography. Example: Susan starts the peel off on count "6," starts kick ball change step on left foot, OR Counts "1–4" kick ball change, counts "5–8" prep double outside left turn.

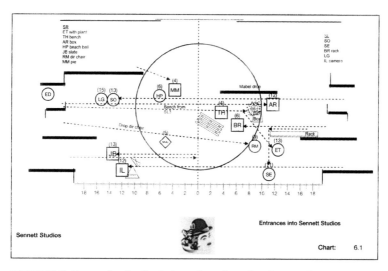

FIGURE 6 *Example of a final chart (based on the chart in Figure 5), using the "Stage Write" App.*

98

"Stage Write" iPad app

Stage Write has recently been dubbed "the new standard of documentation for staging and choreography." Created by Director/Choreographer, Jeff Whiting, who has worked on Broadway for nearly a decade, Stage Write is an iPad app that allows you to easily and accurately document staging and choreography for any [of] size production. It allows you to track the onstage spacing, traffic patterns, prop tracking, moving scenery, quick change locations, and also allows you to enter notes, and document the choreography alongside the counts in the music.

[One of] the greatest things on this app is the point of view switch. Most of the time, people chart from the point of view of the Director. But you can change the point of view by hitting a button. Now the chart is flipped so you feel like you're onstage and you don't have to physically move the iPad upside down.

Stage Write is an essential tool for the Swing because it allows you to keep all of your detailed notes in one place and its portability makes it so easy to carry and keep with you, and refer to before you go onstage. Since its release in early 2012, it has already been embraced by the entertainment community and is currently being used in numerous Broadway, West End, and National Tour productions (*Phantom of the Opera*, *Book of Mormon*, *Les Misérables*, etc.) as well as countless entertainment companies and concerts around the globe. www. stagewritesoftware.com

Jeff Whiting (Choreographer/Director;
Associate Director on over four Broadway shows;
Developer of Stage Write software)

It is also important to make sure that your documentation of formations and Choreography is clear, concise, and makes sense to you. Here are some more notation tips:

● Put counts for Choreography in quotations and give Stage Numbers no quotations. Example: Hit pose on "6" at SL 3. This will help distinguish the two.

- Use/create abbreviations. Example: Cross (X), Left (LF), Right (RH), Stage Left (SL), **Stage Right** (SR), **Upstage** (US), and Downstage (DS).

- To differentiate positions on the number line from positions in the Wings, use no spaces for Wings and add the preposition "In" or "Out." Example: InSL3 denotes a Wing (the third exit on the Upstage side); SL 3 denotes a position on the number line (on the number 3 on the SL side—if using a traditional number line it would be between 2 and 4 on SL).

- Note who is to your left and right. Example: X DS to SL 3, between Mark–SL and Susan–SR on count "6" then exit OutSL2.

Be sure to *always* have a hard copy of your charts at the theatre! If you lose or misplace your iPad or laptop, you will need to make sure you have a back-up plan. Check with Stage Management, as your printing costs may be eligible for reimbursement. Some Swings create one huge binder that has the script, score, and all charts and notation. Others might put the script and score in one binder, then put charts in another and Tracking Sheets or other notation in its own smaller binder. There will be lots of information that you will need to keep organized and accessible.

Tracking Sheets

These are great tools when you need to review a single Track. Instead of looking through every chart, you can condense everything you need to know to get you through a particular Track in a show into two or three pages. This is also the place to store all the other little details you will not want to forget (costume changes, Backstage Tracking, Director's notes, prop information, etc.).

The easiest way to start is to make a template for each Track, listing scenes, musical numbers, and any other basic information you should fill in for each Track.

The template you create can be used as the basis for every Tracking Sheet you need to make. It is easier to delete sections you do not need for a particular Track, plus it may help you double-check that you

Actor Track:

Pg 1

Title of Show: A Swing's Life- The Fictional Musical

M1 TRACK
Pre-Show:
Wig Call Time:
Dresser:

Opening - "Got a Lot of Swinging to Do":
Costume:
Props:
Lines/Cues:
Partner:

Wedge:
Pinwheel:
Fancy Feet Section:
Peel off:
Button:

Exit:

Costume Change:
Dresser:

Scene 2 into "Swing on Over Here"
Costume:
Props:
Lines/Cues:
Partner:

First formation:
Popcorn:
Diamonds:
Serpentine:
Button:

Exit:

Costume Change:
Dresser:

Swing Name: Austin Eyer and Lyndy Franklin - Date

FIGURE 7 *Example of template for Tracking Sheets.*

have all the information you need. We recommend creating drafts of these Tracking Sheets. (In other words, do not spend a week making one perfect Tracking Sheet. Instead, complete a "bare bones" draft of every Track you cover. Then, you can go back one Track at a time and finalize everything.) Having something to go by, in case you are thrown on, is better than nothing!

Be sure to number the pages and put your name on every page, just in case it gets misplaced in the flurry of the show. (During a show, you can give your Tracking Sheet to your Dresser and ask him or her to bring it to your next quick change.) Also, putting a date stamp in the footer of the document will ensure that you always have the most recent version. (See Figure 2—"Example of a Swing's Tracking Sheet" in Chapter 3, for a look at a finalized Tracking Sheet.)

It is a good idea to have a draft of your Tracking Sheet for the first time you are tracking backstage. Leave blank spots where you know you need to add more information. And keep that pencil handy, long after you have "finalized" your notes, as you will learn more about the Track every time you go on or get a note, or when someone new joins the cast.

Notecards

Some Swings might use Notecards in addition to or in place of Tracking Sheets. The information on the Notecard can be either a replica or a condensed version of the Tracking Sheet. You might also put "mini-charts" on your cards, if you need to see a formation for reference.

Notecards are wonderful to have during a show, as they are very portable. We have even known Swings to put them in a small zip-loc bag and pin or tuck into a costume, so that if their Dresser could not carry them, they would have them at the next quick change.

Notecards should be bound. Either purchase the spiral bound stack or punch a hole in the top left corner and loop them through a key ring. Be sure to number your Notecards, in case they become unhooked, and make sure your name is marked on them. Use your Tracking Sheet to create the information on the card. Ideally, you should be able to get all the information you need for a particular scene or number onto one card. If you run out of space, use the back or a second card. Then, start the next scene on a new card. (During a show, once you have reviewed a number, you can flip the card. And when you come back for your next quick change, the information you need to look at will be right on top—no need to scan for where you should start reading next.) (See Figure 3—"Example of a Swing's Notecard" in Chapter 3.)

Learning Music as a Swing

Because you are responsible for learning all or nearly all the vocal parts for each song, it is important to be very alert during music rehearsals. Also, it can be helpful to create a "cheat sheet" to put at the front of your score listing each cast member's name and what vocal part they sing. (You can also add this to your name key in the front of your script or bible.) Then you have a quick reference when you need it.

For rehearsals, a recording device is a *must*. When you need to, talk quietly into your recorder to help you remember what is what. ("Boys Vocal, Measure 22, Chuck is singing tenor, Mike is on the bass line.") Also take good notes in your music. Some find it helpful to highlight different vocal lines in different colors. When you are in an original show and experiencing re-writes, it can be helpful to use small Post-it notes so that they can be transferred to new music, as opposed to rewriting your notes on every new page of sheet music.

Another good method is taking notes on a separate page, outside of the score. For example:

"There is Nothing Like a Swing"
@Measure 22—Chuck—FGA; Colin—CEC

Be sure to prioritize your learning around any solo, duet/trio or featured lines. For choral work, start with the vocal part you are most comfortable with and then work to learn the others. In some lucky cases, Musical Directors are giving Swings the *incredible* gift of a CD or MP3 files with all the vocal parts recorded separately for each song in the show. For any of you Musical Directors out there, reading this book, we *really love* this and would be *so grateful* to always get to

FIGURE 8 *Example of a Swing's notation within a musical score.*

have this! We are hoping that with the ever-advancing technology of this century that this will become a more common practice.

Some thoughts from our Swings about learning music:

> Drill drill drill. I do my best to get the music recorded so that there is some sort of through-line to the part. Meaning, that I can push play and sing the alto line for the entire show . . . rather than having my music recorded in bits. It's challenging to be responsible for different vocal parts. I've learned to decipher for myself the place in the show where it is *imperative* that I am singing the different parts perfectly so as not to disrupt the balance of the show, and I've also learned to find places where I can be more gentle with myself about making mistakes. Of course, I do my best to nail all aspects of the vocal parts . . . but if I'm onstage with a mass of Ensemble members, I'm aware that [my] being on the wrong "3" might be very dangerous to other Actors and in fact really hurt the show. Sometimes [my] taking the soprano note rather than the alto one isn't going to be noticed by anyone but me.
>
> JENIFER FOOTE (*On the Twentieth Century,*
> *The Mystery of Edwin Drood, Rock of Ages,*
> *A Chorus Line, Dirty Rotten Scoundrels*)

> Practice! I had to tape each part, drill it, then match it with the physical movement.
>
> MEGAN SIKORA (*Dracula*)

Learning Lines for Multiple Roles

Again, the multi-colored highlighters can come into play here. When you have multiple characters to learn, coding each one in a different color can help you see the scene better in your script. It is always a good idea to make a key on the front page of your script so that you remember that Aimee is highlighted in yellow and Beth is highlighted in green.

> I'm totally anal about how I keep my script. Each track is written out with differently colored ink, with script pages on the right

and blocking diagrams on the back of each page. Blocking is written in with a ruler so my eye can very easily process what I'm reading.

THOM CHRISTOPHER WARREN (The Lion King,
Once Upon a Mattress)

It is a good idea to request a script that is printed only on one side. That way, you can write or draw Blocking diagrams on the left (or blank) side of your script. Just make sure that, if you are working on a new show (where changes are possible), use post-it notes or something that is easily transferable, in case you are given new pages to your script.

"Scene Partner" app

There is an app that can help Swings to learn their lines more efficiently, called Scene Partner.

Scene Partner is a mobile app for iPhone, iPad, and iPod Touch that helps Actors learn their lines. It uses text-to-speech technology, to turn the text of your play into speech, so that you can listen to just your lines, just your cues, cue/line pairs, or whole scenes. You can also record your lines and merge them with the text-to-speech playback. The app takes old-fashioned voice recording to a whole new level. You can use your own script or choose Publisher e-Scripts offered on the app's webstore. Scripts from Dramatists Play Service and Samuel French can be purchased, while scripts from Music Theatre International and Theatrical Rights Worldwide can be rented for officially licensed productions.

J. KEVIN SMITH (Developer of Scene Partner)

9

Swings as Dance Captains

An added responsibility for some Swings is that of also being hired as the Dance Captain. Dance Captains are generally responsible for maintaining the integrity of the original Choreography of the show.

Often, the Dance Captain will be a Swing for the show as well. There are a couple of important reasons for this. First, and foremost, the Dance Captain needs to have the ability to watch the show in order to note and correct any errors. Since a Swing is not onstage performing every night, this allows time for completion of these duties. Second, it just makes sense for the Dance Captain to be a Swing, as they have to know (or at least have notated) all of the tracks in the show anyway, for their Dance Captain duties. Since they already have the bulk of the knowledge, it seems logical that they would carry out Swing duties as well.

From time to time, there may be a Dance Captain who is a member of the Regular Playing Company (often called an Onstage Dance Captain). However, in those cases, there is usually a Co-Dance Captain or Assistant Dance Captain who also serves as a Swing. Basically, someone in the Dance Captain position must be offstage a fair amount of time, in order to watch the show on a consistent basis.

Duties

Dance Captains/Swings will, of course, assume all of the Swing duties that we have mentioned in this book. But, on top of that, they assume several Dance Captain duties as well.

Documenting the Show

It can vary from show to show, as to who is in charge of this very big job. Sometimes, Associate or Assistant Choreographers may be assigned this task. Otherwise, it could be the Dance Captains who create the Show Bible. (And, even if not completely in charge, the Dance Captains may assist on this.)

The creation of the Show Bible involves recording every moment of the show's Choreography (and sometimes musical or other staging). This can be done in a variety of methods, but is quite similar to the Tracking Sheets and stage charts that we have mentioned previously.

Typically, a Show Bible will have one section of full stage charts for every formation of every number in the show. These are usually labeled with character or Actor initials. There will also be another section with a full notation of the Choreography/Blocking for each number or scene, including a description of the movement, and how it matches to the score or script (with counts, etc.)

Putting this gigantic document together is a painstaking process that can take weeks or even months to complete. Just like the creation of the Swings' notes, it is important to watch and document all of the changes during the Tech and Preview Process and make sure those get incorporated into the Show Bible.

Once it is completed, this document (usually housed in a giant three-ring binder) is an incredibly important and helpful tool for both the Dance Captains and the Swings. It is *the* reference source, when there is a question as to the original spacing or Choreography. For Replacement Swings, it can sometimes be the only glimpse into the original rehearsal process. And it can be an incredible resource when trying to absorb the show as quickly as possible. For the Dance Captain, it is the go-to book for teaching the show to new cast members.

Down the road, the Show Bible may be used to restage the show for additional Companies, National Tours, or Regional Productions. For all of these reasons, it is important that the Show Bible is created with care and attention to detail. It must be thorough, accurate, and easy to understand.

Noting the Show

This is one of the important ways that a Dance Captain preserves the integrity of the Choreography. When "noting the show," the Dance Captain (or DC) observes the show and watches for any Choreography or spacing errors, or notes regarding execution, line, or energy of movement. These notes can be "general" (meaning for the entire cast or Ensemble) or "personal" (for one particular Actor). The DC will record these notes in a personal notebook and then disseminate them to the cast in any number of ways.

General notes can be typed up and posted on the Call Board or in the dressing room or placed at each Actor's dressing station. Personal notes can either be typed and placed at the Actor's dressing station or given verbally to the Actor. Rarely is there a group notes session for these types of Dance Captain notes, unless there is a Full Company cleaning rehearsal (which is scheduled from time to time).

It is important for the DC to observe the show on a fairly regular basis. Once a week is the minimum we recommend. The DC will also want to watch any time a Swing or Understudy is on for a new Track, any time a new cast member is on for the first time, and immediately following any cleaning or brush-up rehearsals with the Creative Team. These are important to watch, as it is the DC's job to help Swings and new cast members ease into new tracks by letting them know what worked and what needs work. And, after Brush-Up rehearsals, it is important for them to watch any changes or notes in action, to make sure they are being made accordingly. Often, when the Choreographer returns to see the show, the Dance Captain may sit and take notes with him/her. Or, the Choreographer may take notes and then give them to the Dance Captain to give to the cast.

It is also important for the DC to watch the show from several vantage points. In addition to watching from the House, a good DC should watch (unobtrusively) from the Wings to make sure the cast is properly observing **Stage Depths**, and any tricky backstage traffic is happening as it should. Just as we recommend with Swings, it is important for Dance Captains to gain permission from Stage Management to be in the Wings, particularly if the backstage area is restricted to performing cast and crew in any way. Also, it is important to be discreet in the Wings, so as not to pressure or distract the Regular Performing cast. It is good for the cast to know they are being observed, to some degree. But a good Dance Captain never wants to appear threatening or overbearing.

Dance Captains may also want to watch from the balcony (great view of formations), or the back of the House. Another great tool is the Stage Manager's infrared camera monitor, usually located at the Stage Manager's calling station. This is a great way to catch transitions that happen in a black-out.

Training New Cast Members

This is the part of the job that any Dance Captain in a long-running show will spend the most time doing. Whether it is a new onstage Ensemble member, new Vacation Swing, additional Track for a current cast member, or helping with one of the new Principal Actors, there is usually someone new to train *all* the time!

This is why the accuracy of the Show Bible is so important. Dance Captains will likely have the new cast member in a one-on-one rehearsal in a studio outside of the theatre, or sometimes onstage. Because the rest of the cast does not report to these rehearsals, the Dance Captain must be able to explain to the Replacement Actor exactly where to go, how to get there, and what steps or staging to do along the way. The visual aid of the stage charts can help the new Actor gain a sense of perspective. For the DC, the stage charts are essential to walking the new Actor through his or her Track.

Most of the time, the Replacements will not rehearse with the Regular Playing Company until their Put-In Rehearsal, so it is important that the DC provides all the important information needed, to make them as comfortable as possible in the Track, so that they are ready to join the rest of the cast. This can also mean that in a run-through of a number, the DC might be playing all the other parts in the show, to help the Replacements get a sense of their relationship to others onstage.

Dance Captains must know how to teach any and every Ensemble (and sometimes Principal) Track in the entire show!

Running Put-In Rehearsals

Along with Stage Management, the DC may also be in charge of running Put-In Rehearsals for Regular Playing Company Replacements and/or Swings going on for the first time in a new Track.

For a full Put-In, the whole cast may be called for a run-through of the entire show for a Replacement in the Regular Playing Company. The DC may run this rehearsal (or it could be Stage Management or an Associate/Resident Director or Choreographer). The DC should be prepared to help the new cast member with any problem areas, and be watching with an eagle eye to make sure that the new Actor is fitting into traffic and formations, as they should. It is also a good idea for the DC to create a list of items to cover in this rehearsal, including what moments need to be simply talked through, walked through slowly, or run full-out and in-tempo.

As we have mentioned, the Swings' Put-In may be very last minute and only last about ten to fifteen minutes. In this case, the DC should find out from the Swings what sections they would like to run. (It is a good idea to have an idea of what they *should* run, in case they are too nervous or stressed to process what they need.) The DC must then take the whole cast (or whoever is called) through each section quickly and efficiently—making sure everyone feels comfortable and prepared and no one is panicked. It can also fall to the DC to know which cast members to call in for this rehearsal. So, it is a good idea to create a document that lists (for each Track) who partners with whom, or any other key moments involving other cast members.

Dance Captains will also be very involved when Cut-Shows and Split-Tracks are being determined. A DC should have a list of all the most important parts of every Ensemble Track—items that cannot be missed from a scene, number, set change, or prop move. When more Actors are out than there are Swings to cover, the DC will meet with Stage Management to decide and document for the cast who everyone will be in each scene for that show. Your list will be crucial for that meeting. (And you *should not* try to do this from memory!) You may also need to call to consult with the Choreographer if there are major changes that would have to be made. (It is a good idea to pre-emptively have a conversation with the Creative Team to start strategizing before anyone starts calling out.) Try to think through different scenarios before they become a last-minute reality.

Running/Assisting with Clean-up Rehearsals

Again, depending on the show/Creative Team, Dance Captains may be asked to either run or assist with clean-up rehearsals for the entire cast. These rehearsals are held every few months to make sure everything is running smoothly and Choreography is kept clean and precise. It can be so much easier to give group notes in this setting because you have the whole group in one place, with no distractions. And, you can run the section being noted, to make sure everyone is taking/understanding the notes. If you are running the rehearsals, you should have a game plan—a list of to-fix moments, ordered strategically, based on the needs of the show. If you are assisting in the rehearsal, you are serving as the Choreographer's right arm and extra set of eyes and ears. Be sure to have your Dance Captain notebook handy to take notes on everything that is covered. And make sure you and the Choreographer have communicated regarding what your role should be in the rehearsal (i.e., how vocal you should be, if there are sections where you should dance instead of watch, etc.) After the clean-up rehearsal, it is a great idea for the DC to create a document recapping all the notes and/or changes covered in the rehearsal. This can be posted on the Call Board or in the Dressing Rooms. The cast will have been given a lot of information and it is nice to give them a visual reminder of what was covered, before they step onstage for the evening's performance.

Lyndy's List

Here are some thoughts and suggestions from my time as a Dance Captain.

1   Position of service—I think it's crucial to think of the Dance Captain's job as a position of service. The cast and Swings will appreciate that you do your very best to make their job easier and make them more comfortable when they are

asked to do something new for the first time. Management will appreciate that you are always looking out for the show's and the cast's best interest. I found that when everyone knows that you are aiming to help them, it makes giving notes a lot easier. Dance Captains should be selfless—putting the needs of the show and the cast above their own.

2   Organizational skills—Being organized is a *must*! Aside from the organization of your regular Swing duties, you must keep a neat and organized bible for the whole show. These skills also extend to time management—for running rehearsals and Put-Ins. And, when the DC is organized, it helps the cast to feel at ease.

3   Giving notes—the "Two Times Rule"—This was a tip from one of my favorite Dance Captains, Tim Santos (with whom I worked in the *Radio City Christmas Spectacular*). He taught me that if you see an error on the part of an Actor, write it down, but don't give the note just yet. Then, watch that part in the next performance and see if it happens again. If it does, then give the note. If it doesn't, then you'll know it was a fluke or that they were already aware of the mistake and corrected it on their own. (No one likes a "micro-managing" DC!!)

4   Giving notes—Know thy audience—I think this is one of the most important (and most difficult) things to learn as a Dance Captain. When giving notes, know that people will receive them differently. This has to do with everything from learning styles to personalities. Some are eager to receive notes, while others do not enjoy getting notes or can be defensive. Some need a very detailed note or a demonstration to know what you mean, while others just need something brief. As you get to know your cast, note the preferences and styles of each person (without saying anything, of course!). And then keep that in mind, when you are giving personal notes. Trust me, it makes a *huge* difference when you approach each Actor in the way they work best. It just goes better for everyone! You can also employ the "good ole' rule" of starting and ending with a positive note. It's always a nice way to get your message across.

5 Wearing different hats—One of the other difficult things about being a Dance Captain is that you have to be a leader among your peers. So, you find yourself wearing different hats. Sometimes you are a cast member, chumming around with your friends. And sometimes you are running a rehearsal or serving as an extension of the Management team. It can be tricky to separate the two, and for the cast to view you in different roles. Another tip from Tim Santos was to physically exit and re-enter a room to help "change hats." For example, you are hanging out between shows in the dressing room and then you need to give some notes. Don't try to segue the conversation about the latest movie you saw into a notes session. It just makes people feel uncomfortable. Instead, find a time to exit the room, gather your notes, and re-enter a few minutes later as the Dance Captain, doing your DC duties. When I tried this, it worked brilliantly. It helps everyone to know when it's social time and when it's work time.

6 The saturation factor—This applies to two things. The first is giving notes. While you must maintain the show, you should try not to saturate the cast with notes all the time. They need time to breathe and grow and not feel like their every move is being analyzed all the time. Try to find the happy medium. The second thing is watching/noting the show. I found that if I watched the show too much, I would get desensitized and miss things. It's important to take some time to not watch, so that you come back with fresh eyes. I like the one to two times per week guideline.

7 One step ahead—Good Dance Captains are always trying to be one step ahead—of everyone. Even though Stage Management checks the Call Board, so should you—in case you are about to do a last-minute swing on for someone who is late. You should be thinking of Plan A, B, and C for all kinds of scenarios for Put-Ins, Cut-Shows, etc. Anticipating needs of new Swings, new cast members, and even those who have been in the show a long time makes you feel pro-active and puts the cast at ease—knowing you are on your game.

Thoughts From the Pros

Being an Assistant and a Dance Captain is not unlike being a Swing—because you have to remember everything—all the versions—where people go. I mean, that's your job! I think that's probably harder if you haven't swung a show. Being a Swing expands your brain.

TONY STEVENS (Director/Choreographer of four
Broadway shows; Swing on *Billy*)

Whatever the Swing needs, you have to help them. That's your job. I think that's really important because, especially on a new show, the Swings are fighting for their lives. If a Swing comes to you and says, "Will you stay after work or work lunch hour with me?" I think it's your job, you can't say no. I totally depend on the Dance Captains. I use them a lot. I think it also makes them feel very powerful.

TARA YOUNG (Associate Director/Choreographer
on ten Broadway shows)

I have been the Dance Captain, and then in an emergency had to go on as a Swing for one section of the show. That can be tricky too. In one instance, I only had to go on for a short section in Act Two. On that evening, I chose to sit in the audience to take notes for Act One. However, since I had my "Dance Captain hat" on and was in the audience taking notes, I totally forgot to get dressed for my Act Two entrance that evening!! Luckily, the show continued without a problem! Needless to say, I felt terrible and was incredibly embarrassed!

PATTI D'BECK (*Applause, Annie Get Your Gun,
The Best Little Whorehouse in Texas, A Chorus Line,
Grease, My One and Only, The Will Rogers Follies*)

I always say it's easier to swing a show when you're a Dance Captain because when you teach somebody a track, you know it. And so once I started doing that, I rarely needed any kind of notes, because you did it so often. I taught the steps so much that I knew where everybody went. I knew numbers. I knew entrances . . . everything. Because, once you teach it, you learn it, it's in your body.

JoANN M. HUNTER (Choreographer of two Broadway shows; Associate Choreographer on three Broadway shows; and Swing on *Chicago*)

When I did *Pajama Game* I was an onstage Dance Captain. What was interesting about that show is that I would get swung out [to watch the show], but I would get swung back in to do "Steam Heat" and then I could watch the rest of the show. I had nothing to do with that decision. It's just how they decided to do it. Not fair to the male Swing, I don't know how he felt about that. He may have been fine with it.

For *Curtains* I was onstage Dance Captain in the out-of-town [tryout]. That was rough. I think that I was in the other rehearsal room quite a bit. So I missed a lot of vocal rehearsals, and a lot of staging rehearsals, because I was in the other room, helping with Rob [Ashford], and his Associate JoAnn M. Hunter. Well Rob Ashford pulled me aside after the closing night party at David Hyde Pierce's house and he said, "You know, everyone is very happy with your work, I want you to continue with the show when it happens in New York as Dance Captain, but I want to give you the option of either being onstage or offstage. It's your choice." I was really grateful and flattered for that opportunity to make that decision for myself. That was very nice. And ultimately I decided that I would be an offstage Dance Captain. I think that both are challenging, and both are fulfilling, but I had been an onstage Dance Captain more than once, and I was ready to be an offstage Dance Captain, and swing the show. I have to know the material anyway. That was my realization.

DAVID EGGERS (*How to Succeed . . ., Billy Elliot, Curtains, Chicago, Saturday Night Fever*)

Personally, as a Dance Captain, the way I approached it was [that] I was always available. I usually try to make [Swings] feel comfortable, especially the first time Swings. I would never, for their first time going on for a track, actually watch the show from the front. I would be backstage. A lot of times they wouldn't need me, but every now and then they did need me backstage ("What's next? What do I do?"). A lot of times, I feel like it made them, and all of the people around them more comfortable, because there was someone to talk to, who knew what was going on—every time that they exited the stage [and] before they went back onstage. I'd be extremely supportive. But there is a point in time where I always turn up the heat, when they go on a couple of times

CLYDE ALVES (*Wicked, Hairspray, Beauty and the Beast*—Toronto)

Other Careers for Swings/Dance Captains

The skill set and experiences of Broadway Swings and Dance Captains can be a great platform for aspiring Choreographers and Directors. Sometimes, this can even be an awakening for an artist who never knew they had this desire. Swinging a show takes the performer out of a singular experience and forces them to look at the show through a wide lens. By studying stage pictures, watching shows over and over, and observing the choices made by various Actors, Swings start to gain a larger understanding of the shape of their play. It can be a wonderful learning tool for those who open their eyes to it.

Dance Captains work closely with the Creative Team and may start to enjoy the process of crafting the show. Many Dance Captains transition to the position of Associate or Assistant Choreographer/Director or Resident Choreographer/Dance Supervisor. Associates, Assistants, and/or Supervisors may help the team with creating staging and Choreography, teaching the show, training Dance Captains, supervising numerous Companies of the same show and checking in to give notes, running clean-up rehearsals, etc. Some of these people may also transition to become Directors or Choreographers themselves. It is a great path, full of very helpful stepping-stones along the way.

10

Swings beyond Broadway

There are many places Swings can work besides Broadway. Now, we will cover some of the similarities and differences for the job of the Swing, outside of the Big Apple.

Universal Swings

These brave souls are usually hired for successful shows that have multiple Companies (Broadway, National Tour, LA Company, Chicago Company, etc.) At any moment, the Universal Swing can be whisked away to cover a vacation, injury, or emergency that comes up in any of the other productions running around the world. In the end, it is more cost effective for a production to hire one or two Universal Swings, than to add more resident Swings to each production.

Universal Swings—What to Watch For

1 Changes in Blocking from Company to Company—Even though they might be performing the same show, there may be slight differences in staging, Blocking, or Choreography and these must be noted by the Swings.

2 Different set design/props—These can also be slightly different in each Company. It is especially important to note this for safety!

3   Blending with the Company (onstage and off)—Jumping in
     to join a cast that has been working together for a long
     time can be tricky!

4   Keeping notes up-to-date—Things change a lot in one
     Company. Keeping up with three or four is even
     tougher.

How Universal Swings are Hired

Universal Swings are relatively new to the Swing family. In fact,
Actors' Equity does not have a special term for them. They are called
Vacation/Temporary Swings in the current Production Contract. We
have found that different shows work with Universal Swings in
different ways. Some are kept on retainer, others return to the
Broadway Company if they are not needed on the road, and others
are only hired as needed for any Company.

The amount of time a Universal Swing spends with one Company
usually averages from one to four weeks. But, the contract can be for
any length (one week minimum).

I am on a standard [Production Contract], as an [Ensemble] Swing.
When no one is sick or hurt and I'm not needed anywhere, I act as
a standby Swing on Broadway, which means I come to every show
at half-hour and if everyone is feeling well, I can leave at places! I
get the standard two weeks' vacation and four personal days that
all other Swing contracts get.

CANDI BOYD (*Jersey Boys*—Universal Swing)

When I was doing more Universal Swing work, it was definitely
harder to plan a vacation or make it back to the city for an audition.
Since I was usually filling in for someone already on a vacation or
injured, it wasn't likely that they'd let me go. Although there were
the rare times that I was in the same Company for six months, and
I was able to make an audition then.

NICKY VENDITTI (*Wicked*—Universal Swing)

I wasn't on a retainer, however *Wicked* was wonderful to their Universals in that they kept you working probably fifty out of fifty-two weeks in the year. Not being tied to a contract left you able to do other jobs and turn down their contracts if something else came your way, yet they always tried to keep [us] working. Best case scenario.

SAMANTHA ZACK (*Wicked*—Universal Swing)

Differences in Staging/Choreography

A Universal Swing is responsible for even more information than a Broadway Swing. On Broadway the show is "frozen" and although it is never easy to cover ten tracks, at least there should not be major changes that would keep someone from having clear notes and a general understanding of their tracks. Broadway Swings also have the luxury of working with the same people each week, therefore having rapport with the cast. On the other hand, being a Universal Swing might be appealing to those who want to shake things up a bit.

In *Jersey Boys* there are three women onstage and one Swing backstage. There are five Companies of *Jersey Boys* that I have covered or am currently covering, making it fifteen different tracks I know! Each Company's version of *Jersey Boys* is very different based on many factors like the size of the stage, the layout backstage, the length of the show, which vocal part each girl sings and which number they dance on, cut lines, costume changes happening in various locations, backstage traffic, actual choreography, etc. *So*, my job is to come into a cast, and whichever role I go on for, the show is no different than if the regular cast was all onstage.

The first thing I do when I get to a new Company is go around and try to say "hi," and catch up with the cast and crew, which helps me get back into the world and energy of that Company. I also always watch the show ASAP, which helps remind me of all the small differences in the onstage show. Finally, we often have Understudy Rehearsals where the Dance Captains and Stage Managers always take extra care to keep me updated. But it *is* live theatre, so no matter how prepared I think I am, I always have to stay alert and aware onstage because there is inevitably a change or different cast member that I'm not aware of and I'll get run over!

CANDI BOYD (*Jersey Boys*—Universal Swing)

Swinging into Different Companies

Joining a Company that is run differently or a cast that has developed their own cliques and their own rhythm can be a challenge. Our advice is to try to be sensitive to the cast you are joining. Avoid being too vocal about your opinion, remember you are somewhat of a guest in their home.

I find that most Companies are very receptive to new blood, or at least someone they maybe haven't seen in a while. It's refreshing. So with that, I aim to take the neutral approach and keep it light. We're all professionals at this level and I think if you can just approach people with a sense of ease it will work in your favor. Also, I think it's important to remember that each Company *is* different both technically and socially. Keep the notes straight, and try not to expect the same energy from people in different Companies.

NICKY VENDITTI (*Wicked*—Universal Swing)

I will say, one of the brilliant things [about] being a Universal Swing is you pop in for a few weeks, everyone is excited to see you, and you get to leave before the drama ensues. Literally, one of the best jobs ever.

SAMANTHA ZACK (*Wicked*—Universal Swing)

Keeping Track of Your Tracks

For Universal Swings, technology can really be their best friend. With advances such as Stage Write, Google Drive, Dropbox, and the Cloud, you can create notes for each Track in *each* Company and then have them with you to reference on your phone, laptop, or iPad. Universal

Swings can digitally share charts and Tracking Sheets with Swings and Dance Captains in each Company. If things change they can message each other or even update the changes in a shared folder or document. That said, it is *always* a great idea to print everything out (one never knows when your devices may fail or go missing). You can leave a hard copy of your bible (along with your Tracking Sheets or Notecards) with each Production Stage Manager and ask them to travel it for you.

Pros, Cons, and Tips from the Universals

I'd say the most difficult part is that it can be hard to really and truly feel a part of any one Company. Because you're hopping around so much, you tend to feel like a visitor and that can be a little unsettling. You never get to say "I'm part of the ___ Company." All of this can also be viewed as a positive. I guess it just depends on my mood at the time.

NICKY VENDITTI (*Wicked*—Universal Swing)

Take good notes! Write everything down, [because] down the line you will forget it! Also, get into all the frequent flyer programs! Finally, let people help you, because their show is more familiar to them than you! Listen to any backstage advice!

CANDI BOYD (*Jersey Boys*—Universal Swing)

Swings on Tour

Life on the road is not for everyone, but it is a great way to travel and gain experience, and it can pay well. The job of a Swing on tour is very similar to that of a Broadway Swing. Equity tours will have the same rules in place as they would on Broadway, though depending on how your show is contracted with Actors' Equity your weekly salary and Swing stipend can vary greatly.

The structure is exactly the same. We have an Understudy run-through once every week or two. Anytime I go into the show I practice my partnering ahead of the half-hour call. For me personally, the ever present anxiety of never knowing when or who I'll be performing is, unfortunately, the same in both cases.

IAN LIBERTO (*Promises Promises, Billy Elliot, How to Succeed . . ., Evita*—National Tour)

Tour Swings—What to Watch For

1 Different venues—In each new city, the configuration of the backstage may be slightly different from the last couple of cities.

2 Close quarters—Actors spend a lot more time all together on the road. Stay healthy because when that weird flu hits, *everyone* will go down. You will also have more of a heads up when someone is going to call out, as well as a better idea of exactly why someone is calling out.

3 Tour drama—Sometimes emotions can run high on the road, so things may become a bit personal or overblown because you are now living with your tour family.

Change of Venue

This may seem obvious, but when you are touring you are constantly changing cities and, thus, performance venues. This is the biggest difference between working as a Swing on Broadway, or the road. On tour, some theatres will be huge, with tons of Wing space. Others may have a tiny backstage area, and may have been built during the turn of the twentieth century. When Wing or crossover space is compromised, significant changes may have to be made. Dressing rooms, quick-change booths, prop tables, and the wig area can be in completely different locations from your last city. Actors may have to enter from a different Wing for a particular scene, because they will not be able to make a fast crossover in this particular theatre.

On the day of your first show in a new city, you will be called to the theatre early for spacing and sound check. Usually your PSM or Dance Captain will have a list of changes (due to venue) for the cast. You will have an opportunity to walk through the space to see where everything is now located and to get acquainted with your new surroundings. Plus, you may have time to talk to local Crew and Dressers about tricky traffic patterns backstage or quick changes.

It's always a good idea to track backstage again if you arrive to a theatre that is drastically different than what you're used to. Try to prepare for your first time in each city and take out as many variables as you can.

> SEAN McKNIGHT (*Anything Goes*—National Tour, *A Christmas Story*—National Tour, *Shrek*—First National Tour)

Your Wardrobe Crew is different every time you go into the show. In some cities that's good and in some it's bad . . . I mean Bad.

> IAN LIBERTO (*Promises Promises*, *Billy Elliot*, *How to Succeed* . . ., *Evita*—National Tour)

Calling Out on the Road

Whether on Broadway or on the road, how often the cast calls out is usually based on one thing—the cast itself. This can depend on many variables, including the cast's work ethic, or how taxing the show is, physically.

I find that people don't call out as much on the road so there's a lot more off time. Maybe it's because you have less of a "real life" on tour so there's less temptation to call out when you're not actually ill or injured, or maybe it's because the salary on the road (for most companies) is less and so there's a reluctance to give up that extra eighth of your pay check.

> IAN LIBERTO (*Promises Promises*, *Billy Elliot*, *How to Succeed* . . ., *Evita*—National Tour)

I think one of the days that went down in history was re-blocking *Mary Poppins* three times on a Sunday morning on tour. The phone calls kept creeping in with more and more people calling out, while people were out on vacation and personal days. The show culminated with all of us Swings weaving back and forth. I found myself between four tracks making appearances as men (even partnering women). Then the evening show arrives and one person decides to come back to work for the second show of the day and it shifts everything for all of us Swings. Bleh! Poor Wardrobe!

> ELIZABETH EARLEY (*Something Rotten, Whistle Down the Wind*—National Tour, *Mary Poppins*— First and Second National Tour)

On my first tour, fourteen years ago, it was rare for the Swings to be on. We loved when they were because it was something out of the norm. However, I now find that more often than not, at least one Swing is onstage on a nightly basis. We've become masters at double and triple tracking. Once (while standing in costume waiting to go on) a cast member looked at me and said, "Must be nice not to be on." I looked at him with confusion and said "I'm on right now . . . in a girl's track, like I was yesterday." His response, "Yeah, that doesn't count."

While on tour with *Shrek*, we seemed to be playing the snow belt in the worst possible time . . . winter. We got to Buffalo, and the weather didn't disappoint. It was freezing, covered in snow, and the cast was sick. On Opening Night we had seven people out of the show and an eighth was only there because another fellow Swing and I bribed him to stay. We were truly pushing the limits of how the show was going to be performed that evening. When the review came out the next day it said "A testament to the strength of the touring Company would be the fact that we saw no fewer than seven Replacement Actors last night in a Company that only employs five Swing (or substitute) performers. You would never have known" (Anthony Chase, ArtVoice). It was nice to be recognized for blending in.

> SEAN McKNIGHT (*Anything Goes*—National Tour, *A Christmas Story*—National Tour, *Shrek*—First National Tour)

Close Quarters

Another major difference in swinging on the road is that you are with your road Company "24/7." Not only do you share the theatre and dressing space, but also buses, planes, and hotels. On Broadway,

Actors are in their own homes. They have "extracurricular" activities to fill their days and loved ones to be with at night. On the road, your days might be filled with sight-seeing with your cast mates, you take your meals with your cast mates—you may even room with a cast mate.

Swinging on the road is very personal. Because you always know where everyone is and what they are doing, when someone calls out you are more likely to know why they are doing it. You just have to remind yourself that it's your job to go on regardless of why they called out. Don't take it personally if someone calls out or doesn't call out. Your job is to be there when someone does call out.

MICHAEL BIREN (*Billy Elliot*—Second National Tour, *A Funny Thing Happened on the Way to the Forum*, Regional—Goodspeed Opera House)

The sheer fact that you are living, traveling, and working together changes the dynamic. Your work colleagues become more like family. They are not only your scene partners, they are your confidants, wingmen, day trip buddies, etc. Because you get to know them so intimately you can easily begin to read/predict behavior. It can be blatant, like somebody packing-up their station after Saturday night's performance or something more along the lines of knowing that someone is flying back to New York for a final callback, or witnessing a cast mate injure himself [while working out], or having breakfast with the star and noticing that she has lost her voice. On tour, it is often finding out that someone hasn't called out that is more surprising than hearing that you are on.

SEAN McKNIGHT (*Anything Goes*—National Tour, *A Christmas Story*—National Tour, *Shrek*—First National Tour)

Thoughts from the Pros on Broadway Versus Touring

I like the job the same. The lifestyle of a Tour Swing versus a Broadway Swing is something that I cycle through in terms of preference. If you are not someone who travels well, then tour is a tough life. But I loved touring and loved traveling the country. Sometimes I wish I was back on the road enjoying the sights and sounds of new cities. Other times I prefer having a more stable gig where I go home to my own house every night! I love being a homebody back in NYC. But the job is basically the same for me.

> NATHAN SCHERICH (*Jersey Boys*—Broadway and National Tour)

I prefer swinging in New York. It's better to have all the free time a Swing has when you're in your own city and can take on extracurricular activities, it's harder to do that on tour. Plus if you have a particularly rough show it's nice to grab a beer at your favorite bar and find comfort in your own living space.

> IAN LIBERTO (*Promises Promises*, *Billy Elliot*, *How to Succeed . . .*, *Evita*—National Tour)

Deciding to go on the road might seem like a no-brainer, but to do so means to leave your entire personal life behind. Though technology has made life a lot easier, you are still leaving your spouse, family, friends, and home behind. Depending on the tour schedule, you are also removing yourself from the field for possible future work. Flying back to NYC for an audition is costly and often impossible. Touring has so many benefits, but nonetheless a commitment that requires a sacrifice to one's personal life. To choose to do so without the guarantee of being onstage every night is something that not everyone can handle.

> SEAN McKNIGHT (*Anything Goes*—National Tour, *A Christmas Story*—National Tour, *Shrek*—First National Tour)

Swinging Regionally and in Las Vegas

There are two other venues where you might land a job as a Swing in the States. Most contracts, outside of Production Contracts and basic touring contracts, do not require a Swing. However, many productions that have a large Ensemble, heavy dancing, or long runs might employ at least one female and/or one male Swing.

Regional Swings

Some short-running regional or summer stock theatres may hire a Swing as an insurance policy for the show. They are not very likely to go on, but when they do the Company is glad they hired them!

Regional Swings—What to Watch For

1 Payment—If the Company is not required to have a Swing, chances are you will not receive a Swing stipend or any add-ons (unless you are an Understudy or dance captain).

2 Rehearsals—Your rehearsal process is very short, and you may not have many (if any) Understudy Rehearsals.

3 (Not) going on—The chances that you will actually go on may be slim. You may feel like you have to do a lot of work, without ever going on.

We, at Goodspeed, engage Swings because they are essential:

1 To maintain the artistic integrity of the production

2 To keep the curtain up

3 And because it makes economic sense: i.e., one salary against refunding an entire House certainly is a no-brainer.

In many ways we look for the most accomplished dancers as Swings: After all, they do "swing" many tracks in the production, and sometimes are Understudies as well. There is no question that talent and flexibility are at the top of our list of considerations.

MICHAEL PRICE (Executive Director of
Goodspeed Musicals, Connecticut)

I've worked, regionally, where the Dance Captain has to pick up the slack if someone is sick or injured, or they bring in a temporary Replacement. But my first Swing job was for *Forum* at Goodspeed, where they, more often than not, employ two Swings for each show. Swinging regionally on short runs tends to be boring because there isn't a huge chance you are going to go on. I didn't go on until the last week of performances. It's just a much more truncated process, so you have to be a little more on your game as far as going on is concerned. Also, depending on how good the Stage Manager is at calling for Understudy Rehearsals, you might not have a lot of rehearsals, so you just have to make sure you really follow along during Tech and keep up your shadowing.

MICHAEL BIREN (*Billy Elliot*—Second National Tour, *A Funny Thing Happened . . .*—Goodspeed)

Vegas Swings

If you like all the fancy nightlife that Vegas has to offer, plus shorter shows, Vegas swinging is the way to go!

Vegas Swings—What to Watch For

1   Shorter shows—Shows will be cut down to about ninety minutes, with no intermission. You may only have seven shows a week!

2   No matinees—Most shows have no matinees. For example, your show schedule might look something like this: Tuesday 6:30 p.m. and 9:30 p.m., Wednesday–Friday 7:00 p.m., Saturday 8:00 p.m. and Sunday 8:00 p.m.

3   The VIP treatment—Extra benefits may be offered, such as catered meals, special events, and invitations to restaurants or clubs.

Doing *Jersey Boys* in Vegas came with many perks. For example, on two-show days, we were fed because of the quick turnaround of our show schedule. Also, there were no matinees in Vegas. Lots of opportunities for press and fun events with other casts like bowling nights, softball, and various social get-togethers were very common. Also, I remember that we were treated well wherever we went. Vegas is all about hospitality. So, there were many benefits to performing in the town. Access to clubs, great restaurant experiences, and semi-celebrity status were all something that was unique to the experience. Also, the shows were all ninety minutes or less because the hope is to get audiences back into the casinos as quickly as possible. I loved doing *Jersey Boys* in Vegas. The cast, crew, and everyone involved were a pleasure to work with. One of the best experiences of my life.

ANDREW FRACE (*Jersey Boys*—Vegas)

Vegas shows are shorter and faster, so quick changes are faster. Some Vegas shows don't have matinees, but still eight shows, so no turnover time if you've got to do two different tracks in a day. We'd get out of mics, throw on robes, shovel down a buffet they put out in the green room, and then start getting dressed again. Vegas has industry nights . . . a lot. So casts out there get to walk the red carpets and get bottle service and such.

COLIN TRAHAN (*Jersey Boys*—Broadway,
Vegas, National Tour)

Swings Abroad—in the United Kingdom, Germany, and Australia

Swings are not confined to one continent. Anywhere there are long-running commercial musicals, Swings will be found. Swings work in the United Kingdom (UK), Germany, and Australia and can be found in international touring productions in places like Japan, China, New Zealand, Canada, and the Netherlands, to name a few.

Varying Factors from Country to Country

1   Respect for the Swings—Some countries still have the stigma that the role of the Swing is second best. Some others are ahead of the curve, making sure that the Swings are well taken care of.

2   Compensation—Sometimes the Swings make more than the Regular Playing Company (or as it is known abroad,

"the First Cast") and sometimes there is no weekly Swing
stipend.

3 Different union rules—Actors' Equity has certain rules in
place for Swings, regarding costumes, wigs, pay rates, etc.
But other countries may have slightly different rules or they
may not even have an Actors' Union at all, leaving the
decisions to the Producers of each show.

We asked International Swings what makes the experience as a
Swing abroad different from swinging in the US:

In Germany, the money is better for Swings than for First Cast
Ensemble. In England it was exactly the opposite. In Germany, the
Swings are generally onstage every single day, off-shows are very
rare, whereas in England, the First Cast tend to be more reliable
so that the Swings are not always needed. In Germany, they
employ a much larger team of Swings for each show than in
England, about ten Swings for an Ensemble of fourteen or so, and
Cut-Shows are very normal. I never experienced a Cut-Show in
England. In Germany, I feel that Swings are in general much more
respected and valued as they tend to be the more able, versatile,
and reliable artists who are onstage every night and holding the
show together, whereas in England they tend to be seen as the
second choice cast who don't go onstage as often. In Germany,
Swings have to go onstage in much more last-minute, sometimes
quite chaotic, circumstances, due to last-minute changes, and
Swings find themselves feeling quite under-rehearsed when they
have to perform. It is very unlikely that a Swing will get anywhere
near the same rehearsal time as the First Casts did, and they can
be lucky if they get a Put-In. I felt that in England there were far
less emergency situations and I tended to get more rehearsal
before being thrown onstage.

Germany has very different sick regulations. You can be sick for
up to six weeks, and still receive full pay. You only need a sick note
after three days' absence. As a result, people do call in sick more.
Therefore when casting a show in Germany, it is vitally important

to have a good, strong team of Swings. In England, calling in sick is not something that people tend to do very often, certainly not for small aches and pains or colds or whatever. Calling in sick, in England, often leads to a bad reputation, and employers and colleagues have less understanding and tolerance for that sort of thing. As a result, there are a lot less absences and a less urgent need for Swings (or at least not as many).

England's theatrical business is far more competitive. There are more productions and more artists, [so] people tend to accept conditions that people wouldn't necessarily accept in Germany. For this reason, I think that artists are more protective of their own roles, they are less keen to allow a Swing or a cover perform for them because they seem to be more aware of the competition than in Germany.

Germany's working laws tend to be a little more oriented to the well-being of the worker rather than the employer, which is great for the employees but can lead to complacency amongst the artists and staff. The cast feels very secure in their contracts and they know they will be taken care of because there are lots of rules in place to protect them, so they are less concerned about losing their jobs or being replaced or consequences of a bad reputation, etc.

LUCY COSTELLOE (*Tanz der Vampire*—Germany, *Dirty Dancing*—Germany, *Singing in the Rain*—UK)

The job is different to America, in that Swings in Germany are on for all of their tracks all the time. This is due to the fact that in a year contract, everyone has approximately six weeks' vacation time and sick days are paid (and somewhat unlimited). This means that between coverage during vacation time and people actually staying home when they are sick, Swings play all of their tracks continuously.

HOLLY HYLTON (*Phantom of the Opera*—Germany)

I think the only difference in swinging in other countries is the restriction of what you are able to do during the period of learning the tracks you are required to know. I know that in some countries, filming of the rehearsals and the show is forbidden so the learning process is a lot harder and more time consuming as you aren't able to film something and then go back over and over it to notate the individual tracks.

DARREN CARNALL (*Ghost*—UK, *Viva Forever*—UK, *Dirty Rotten Scoundrels*—UK)

The biggest difference I would say from London to NYC from a swinging point of view is that even though the payment is exactly the same, the Producers I have been lucky enough to work with, here in NYC, really have taken care of the Swings. From including them on the cast album, Tonys performances [to] publicity, etc., which I never take for granted, as they don't have to do that and I know it has always meant the world to me. I will always feel strongly that the Swing payment in all countries is nowhere near what it should be. And that's not about being greedy, it's simply about being fair, the Swings' workload is simply massive. But a lot of the Swings I have known over the years are the ones, also for the most part, that become Creatives in their own right. [They] go on to become Teachers, Choreographers, Directors, and have beautiful long careers.

SARAH O'GLEBY (*Promises Promises*, *How to Succeed* . . ., *Saturday Night Fever*—Germany and UK, *Mamma Mia!*—UK, *We Will Rock You*—UK, *A Funny Thing Happened* . . .—UK, *Footloose*—UK, *Candide*—UK)

The treatment whilst in performance of the Scandinavian tour was not quite the same as the UK, or acceptable, as I wasn't even provided with my own costumes—often having to wear other people's costumes in order to go on to perform.

EMMA WOODS (*Cats*—UK, *Copacabana*—Scandinavian Tour, *Mary Poppins*—UK, *Sister Act*—UK)

I have been a Swing in three countries, Germany (I had to sing in German), my country of birth in New Zealand, and in Australia where I met my husband. In Germany (which was some time ago for me), all [of the] Ensemble cast were on roughly the same wage and Swings performed five shows a week minimum. The production gave every First Cast performer a mandatory show off on the weekends to reduce injury. They had $20 masseuses on the weekends . . . very advanced thinking for those times and it worked out well for all. The Swings were kept up to pace on all the subtle changes and the cast got to take care of themselves. I never experienced that kind of common care for all again. The cast was international and respected all. We were like a large family as everyone was in Hamburg, Germany for one reason only. I was always treated well by the Creative Team. The only time I had a bit of a challenge was in Australia—I think that was due to the naturally competitive spirit of the nation which isn't a bad thing if directed in the right way.

NICOLA HUMPHREY (*Cats*—Germany/Australia/
New Zealand, *Sesame Street Live*—UK)

In Australia, due to budget constraints, usually not enough Swings are hired to cover the cast. In my case I was hired as a Swing [for] all the five female [Actors], which included learning all three vocal lines—plus first cover lead role, second cover supporting lead, and second cover supporting role—with Dance Captain thrown in on top. This was massive! There is more and more expectation being thrown to Swings, I hope they are given the support they need. We don't have mandatory vacation days. In most companies you can't take vacation for the first twelve months of the contract. Other companies are more liberal and encourage time off, but it is not mandatory. We are allowed to film, but only for ourselves. Obviously, no one else is allowed to see it. Generally women only cover female tracks and men cover male tracks, but in my experience, in absolute days of chaos and Split-Tracking this has been saved by drag appearances!!

LISA SONTAG (*The Addams Family*—Australia)

To be honest, I think it's very similar. I would have to say though, that it was particularly more stressful on Broadway. In Australia, we had a spacing call pretty much anytime a Swing went on for a new or different role. On Broadway, there weren't always spacing calls—there usually wasn't time! It is more stressful, swinging on Broadway, because of the half-hour call rule—you can call in at the half, and say you won't be coming in. For Australia, you must call in by 4:00 p.m. on a weekday and (I think) 11:00 a.m, on a matinee day. This rule was great for Swings. Sure, there were the exceptions. Accidents happen, last minute sickness, etc. But generally, if cast members called in by these times, you would have loads of time to space out your show, arrive early to the theatre, do your makeup or costume/prop preparation, before you had a spacing call. It took *so* much of the stress and pressure off. On Broadway, you found out at the half. And if there was a spacing call, you barely had time to do a warm-up or gather your thoughts! Having said that, you got used to it, made it work, and got very good at being super quick at looking at your notes and executing them. Swinging in Australia was awesome. We did have an American team rehearsing our show, so we were treated the same way a Swing on Broadway would be treated. In Australia, any wage is up for negotiation, it is usually taken into account your past experience and how much the Producers want you! I want to say I got paid the same or very similar when I was swinging *Chicago*, whether I was onstage or off. There was maybe a very small incentive per show if we went on.

DEONE ZANOTTO (*A Chorus Line*,
Chicago—Australia and Asia)

Having swung [in Australia] twice in my career, both experiences were vastly different. *Cats* was my first Swing experience. This was difficult, but so rewarding. I was one of two Swings who hadn't swung before and the other Swings were existing cast members. Their help and knowledge was incredible. We really looked after each other. We were very well supported by the cast and creatives and my fee reflected that. I later moved into a role within the show and have since always had the utmost respect for Swings. They are the glue.

The second time I swung was in *Rock of Ages*. The American Creatives who cast me were so respectful and enthusiastic about "team swing" throughout the audition and rehearsal period. After they left though, the experience for me, personally, became difficult and, as the season wore on, somewhat strained. Although I had wonderfully creative experiences, a culture began where Swings were being noted by more departments than the resident directorial team. Thus began a culture where, at times, the Swings felt unsupported and for me, personally, this was an unhealthy state of mind. I worked so hard and was on so much for so many roles, but was left feeling disappointed and underwhelmed by the whole experience. I made a decision after *Rock of Ages* that I would never swing again. Although I felt I was good at it, it became abundantly clear that, for me, being onstage nightly is a priority.

JOHN O'HARA (*Cats*—Australia, *Rock of Ages*—Australia)

Tips from the International Swings

I would warn them about the lack of rehearsal and lack of attention the Swings get during the production of the show, and advise them to attend as many First Cast rehearsals as possible to get as much first-hand information as they can. I would tell them to keep their eye on the Choreographer at all times because they tend to make changes without letting Swings know. Swings in Germany need to be brave and extremely sensitive to colleagues. Once they have performed in these conditions, they'll feel ready for anything!

LUCY COSTELLOE (*Tanz der Vampire*—Germany, *Dirty Dancing*—Germany, *Singing in the Rain*—UK)

Know your material! You might feel able to "wing" it as a Swing but the rest of the Company won't thank you for it. They need to feel as confident in you as you do. Equally, you should be allowed to have your own interpretation of a role, not a carbon copy. The job should require you to hit the mark, say the right line at the right time or with the right harmony but how you portray a role can still be your own . . . own it!

EMMA WOODS (*Cats*—UK, *Copacabana*—Scandinavian Tour, *Mary Poppins*—UK, *Sister Act*—UK)

Summing It Up

Wherever you find a successful, long-running musical, you are bound to find a hard-working Swing team. The differences mentioned above mostly boil down to the Union in each country that handles the

Swings' contracts, or the company that is producing the musical. Around the world, the job is basically the same. And, it seems universal that Swings crave support from their Creative Team and cast. While we could write a whole book about swinging in each of these countries, we hope you enjoyed this glimpse into the world of swinging internationally and across America.

11

Swing Stories

Any Broadway Actor will tell you, there is nothing more fun than hearing the "war stories" of those who have treaded the boards before and with them. What is even more fun is hearing all the crazy antics of the Broadway Swings. And, on that note, we have compiled our favorite Swing stories. From awe inspiring to embarrassing or just downright hilarious, these delicious memories of swinging on Broadway deserve to be told!

Lyndy Franklin Smith

I was hired to be a Replacement Swing in *The Little Mermaid*. The three female Swings were assigned first, second, and third covers—an awesome way to come into a show! In my rehearsal period, we focused on my first and second covers, with the idea that once I was officially in the show (i.e., when I was in the building during performances), I would continue learning my third covers. (Easy enough, right?) By my first day "in the building," I had learned four of the eight tracks I would cover. I was also assured that my first week in the show, I would not be put on, as my costumes and wigs were not ready and I had not been taught the makeup plots yet. (Famous last words.) My second show "in" was a Wednesday matinee. Sure enough, right around noon, I got a call from Stage Management. Three women had called out of the show (meaning I needed to go on, or it would be Split-Track time for the other Swings). And, of course, the three women out were three of the four tracks I had not learned yet. I remember the Stage Manager saying, "Which of these do you think you could get through?" Quickly, I decided to go with a track that was fairly similar to my first covers, in that she was in many of the same numbers, so it would just be a matter of spacing. I already knew the steps. I also told the Stage Manager that I had not had my makeup lesson (the makeup for *Mermaid* was very intricate), nor had I been able to do backstage tracking for this track (the backstage traffic at *Mermaid* was also very intricate). So, I asked if an Assistant Stage Manager could meet me at each of my exits and take me safely to my next entrance, and mentioned that I would need help with all my makeup changes during the show. She said, "No problem, we will get you whatever you need."

I raced to the theatre and arrived with about an hour until the show started. I sat in the makeup chair as someone fit a wig to my head, and applied my makeup. I had the Dance Captain's Show Bible in my lap and my fellow Swing, Julie Barnes, talked me through the track as I attempted to scribble some sort of cheat sheet, with numbers and spacing, to take with me backstage. Then, I was sent quickly to Wardrobe, where they were working feverishly to get the alterations completed on my costumes, to a point where I could perform in them. That fitting seemed to take forever, as all I wanted to do was go over the track. I was running numbers in my head and humming harmonies all the while. After a brief Put-In, I had about ten minutes to dress, collect myself, and take a deep breath. Just then, the overture began. Ready or not, here we go!!

The rest of the performance is pretty much a blur. Somehow, some way, I made it through with no major disasters. (Well, except that my "mer-tail" fell off near the end of "She's In Love." What do you do in that case? Pick up your tail and exit Stage Right!) I'm not sure if I took another deep breath until the curtain call, but I will say that it is one of my proudest performing moments. After successfully going on in a Broadway show, in a track you really haven't learned yet, you feel like you can accomplish anything!

LYNDY FRANKLIN SMITH
(*The Little Mermaid, A Chorus Line*)

J. Austin Eyer

My very first show as a Swing, *Curtains*, was a great learning experience. During the end of Act One, there is a moment (that can always be found in a Rob Ashford show) where this huge transition happens in just one eight-count phrase. The boys grab their chairs and run Upstage; the girls leap onto the chair and up onto the bar; then the boys get rid of the chair and run back downstage. Well, on this particular show the wonderful Mary Ann Lamb was my dance partner. I ran Upstage, put my chair in place, held out my hand, and right as she leapt onto the chair it flipped and down she went. It all happened so fast. I still, to this day, don't know how it happened or if I could have done anything to prevent the situation in the first place. She slammed her shin onto the front of the bar. I was mortified and spent the rest of the number (and the week) replaying that moment over and over in my head. What had happened?! Of course Mary Ann, without missing a beat, pulled herself up on the bar like nothing happened, so I kept going. In the next section I could tell she was not okay. We were doing our partnering and she was bleeding onto the stage and was starting to favor her other leg. I kept asking, "Are you ok?" and she kept nodding. Well, the curtain came down at the end of Act One and the Stage Manager made the call to send her to the hospital. When the show finished and after everyone left, I sat in my dressing room and cried. I felt so bad. If I had injured myself onstage, I could have dealt with that, but if you are somehow involved with someone else's injury, you feel horrible. I heard a knock on the dressing room door and there was my Production Stage Manager, Beverley Randolph. She asked, "How are you doing?" I told her how awful I felt, and how I wished that, in the moment, I could have done something to prevent it. She sat down next to me, put her arm around me and said, "What we do is a sport. You all are athletes. And from time to time people are going to get injured. You have to be at peace with that, do your job and let it go. It wasn't your fault. It was an accident and Mary Ann is going to be fine." Bev was amazing and made me feel so much better. I hope that all Swings are fortunate enough to have a Production Stage Manager like Beverley in their corner, fighting for them.

When I started as a Swing in *Mermaid*, I had a much better sense of what I was stepping into. During my first week "on" in the show I went on for three different (unscheduled) tracks. One of the tracks was a flying fish and a bird in the show, which meant we flew around in these spinning pods of death. In these numbers, there was some very basic choreography, which of course I hadn't been taught yet. As I'm being strapped into the pod for the first time, the Assistant Stage Manager ran over and said to me, "Just watch what the other people are doing onstage and follow them. Oh, and did anyone tell you about lowering your head while you're spinning?" I said "No." He said, "Oh, this is really important. Make sure every time you complete a rotation that you lower your head. Otherwise your headpiece (this large fish-head with fabric) will get caught in the machinery and that would be *very* bad." I had no idea what he meant. So, every two seconds (when I wasn't watching my other cast mates for the choreography) I would duck my head just to make sure my fish-head didn't get caught! I'm sure I looked ridiculous but my head was intact when I left the stage.

J. AUSTIN EYER (*How to Succeed . . .,
The Little Mermaid, Curtains*)

Mark S. Hoebee

My favorite Swing story has to do with *Victor/Victoria*. I had actually left the show several months earlier and was working on a directing gig when one day I got a phone call from the Production Stage Manager, Bonnie Becker, who said that they were desperate. They were down four guys, I think, and one of the Swings was on vacation. She asked if I would come back and do the show. I had been out of the show for at least four months and I had no time to rehearse or prepare. I said I would come back if I could create my own track and do the slots that I knew I could remember with no rehearsal. Bonnie said yes. So I finished my rehearsal and ran to the theatre. I got there just before half-hour and had a few minutes onstage to reacquaint myself and warm up. I was so busy getting ready I didn't have time to even say hello to most of the Company. Well, apparently no one told Julie [Andrews] that I was back and going on. It was the top of the "Jazz Hot" number and there is a moment where Julie would lie back on the top of the piano and lean right into Arte's chest while singing ". . . don't ever let it end. . . ." Well, when she did this move and noticed it was me, that night she sang ". . . don't ever let it end—oh! Hello Mark!" I am sure the audience didn't fully understand, but most of the cast was in hysterics. It was heaven.

MARK S. HOEBEE (*Victor/Victoria*, *Beauty and the Beast*, *Nick & Nora*, *Jerome Robbins' Broadway*)

Jody Reynard

I was on for a track where I had a lot of technical things to do; one of which was drive a golf cart. It was my first matinee in a while in this track and I was really nervous about driving the cart for some reason. I made my entrance in the cart and when I made my first stop, an Actor fell off the back. I tried to put that out of my head, because the next part of the drive included picking up the title character and driving them around for bit. I remember getting them safely off the back of the golf cart and I also remember vaguely thinking, "Don't drive off the edge of the stage," and WHAM!!! I run smack into the proscenium. The show didn't stop, as several cast members and I tried to get the golf cart in a position to be driven offstage. That didn't work. So several Crew members then maneuvered onto the stage to try and get it moving—all the while the show is still going on. Finally a props guy gets the cart offstage and the show still went on. I definitely perked up that matinee audience and I'm still expecting the whole experience to end up on YouTube.

JODY REYNARD (*Legally Blonde*, *Taboo*, *Fosse*)

Jason Snow

Once during *The Music Man* I was put on for the youngest (ten years old) female Ensemble member. I wasn't costumed as a young girl but still found throughout the course of the show many a moment when I was "stretching" the boundaries of believability by acting so "young" in certain scenes. The part was directed to be awfully precious. Well . . . at the button [end] of the big River City townspeople production number, "Iowa Stubborn," the "young girl" was to end up sitting alongside Harold Hill on his suitcase. At the time, TV Actor Eric McCormack had recently joined the Company as Professor Harold Hill, and apparently hadn't been informed of the switch happening on this particular performance. When we hit the button position and he turned to give the "young girl" his "reaction" to finding her on his suitcase, he completely froze with the widest eyes I've ever seen, shocked to find instead a fully grown young man by his side. He couldn't help but laugh for a quick second, but soon went on with things as per usual. His initial reaction was priceless. His quick recovery was a testament to always being present and rolling with the punches onstage.

JASON SNOW (*The Little Mermaid, The Music Man, Hairspray*)

Karl Christian

In the opening scene of *Beauty & The Beast*, the song "Belle," the main character walks through the village and encounters all the local townspeople in little vignettes. I think there are six mini scenes within the song. Once in the dead of winter, four out of the eight men in the Ensemble of *Beauty and the Beast* are out sick. The In-Out sheet is a mile long. We used to call it an "all skate." Andrea McCardle [the original "Annie" on Broadway] is Belle. I walked into half-hour and caught her at the door and she said, "Looks like it's just you and me out there, kid. Have fun." So Andrea McCardle and I pretty much did the entire opening scene together, just the two of us. She would talk to me as the baker, say hello to a female character (while I did a quick change offstage while singing), [then she'd] talk to me as the bookseller, talk to a female character, talk to me as the butcher, talk to a female character, and so on. It was like doing an Understudy Rehearsal for a full paying audience. We sort of smirked our way through it. It was so ridiculous, and pointless to be nervous or overwhelmed. I remember thinking, "Anything I do is better than nothing, there are no men onstage except me!" I had my own little two-man show with Little Orphan Annie.

One of my worst Swing moments was learning that making an entrance at even a slightly wrong moment can have enormous consequences. In the second act of *Miss Saigon* there is a scene known as "The Nightmare." It's a chaotic recollection of the last days of the Vietnam War. Strobe lights, lots of onstage traffic with people and sets moving in the dark. I'm carrying an M16 over my shoulder. I entered maybe ten to fifteen seconds too early and ran the butt of my gun right into the face of Kim (the lead). She immediately starts gushing blood. I'm a wreck because there's nothing I can do. Joan Almedilla, being the person she is, finished the show and was ultimately ok. In fact when I went to apologize after the show she was the one who ended up comforting me. So maiming the star of your show is not what you dream about, when you grow up hoping to dance on Broadway.

KARL CHRISTIAN (*Miss Saigon,*
Beauty and the Beast, Jumpers)

Paula Leggett Chase

I was responsible for all the women's tracks in *Kiss Me, Kate,* which featured an Ensemble of wildly varying shapes, sizes, and skill sets and since there was a lot of partnering involved (and at 5-foot-9-and-a-half inches tall, I'm usually the maypole in any cast I'm in, with exception of *Crazy for You*), that presented some unique challenges as well as a source of hilarity for the entire Company. When I went on for the lovely and oh-so-wee JoAnn M. Hunter, everyone who was not onstage gathered in the wings to watch me be partnered by the wonderful Jerome Vivona, who just so happens to top out in height somewhere around my shoulders. Jerome and I didn't care one bit if we were more "Too Darn Funny," than the intended, "Too Darn Hot," we had a great time and we actually danced very well together.

PAULA LEGGETT CHASE
(*Dirty Rotten Scoundrels, Kiss Me Kate*)

Tripp Hanson

Many times in *Kiss Me Kate*, I had to do a split of a singer/ dancer track. In the delicious number celebrating the wine festival, "Cantiamo d'Amore" (We Sing of Love), I had to cover for a dancer who had to help one of the dancer women [into] the wine vat. This particular dancer was certainly as tall as me, and all muscle! Solid as a rock. It's a slow, sensual moment . . . in theory. There's been a sexy lead up to the moment . . . lowering her gently to the ground . . . removing her shoes one at a time, slowly peeling her stockings off . . . a heated lift to bring her into my arms, her legs wrapped around my waist . . . walk her to the vat, and set her up on the edge. . . . We were really good to this point! Feeling it! Hot, sexy, flirty. . . . At this point, we were to change hand positions, in order that she could fan [kick] her upstage leg over my head, and slowly turn into the vat to begin the grape stomping dance. . . . Wellllllllllll . . . I don't know what happened exactly! Like most of these moments in Swing life (mine, anyway), things are going really well, until they're not, and suddenly the movie goes into slow motion as the vehicle begins spinning out of control on the ice. . . . Our hands were (apparently!) tangled, and instead of turning slowly . . . she went legs akimbo, and fell backwards into the vat, incredibly Lucy Ricardo! The audience gasped, as did I. And from the bottom of the vat, her microphone in perfect working order, you heard a voice, giggling: "You are so fired."

There's one other . . . *Drowsy Chaperone*. I had been on a few times, and was feeling pretty good about this one. . . . The opening number of the show is a hugely intricate, carefully timed number, introducing the entire cast of the "record album" of the show within a show. . . . As the number ends, the cast is called to dinner (or drinks more likely, given the show . . .) by the butler (the inimitable Edward Hibbert), and thus the stage clears, leaving "Man In Chair" (the also inimitable Bob Martin) to carry on with his story to the audience. I had been collecting various props as planned, suitcases, coats, etc., and had re-entered on cue, just in time to open the door for the cast to file out in a beautifully orderly fashion, as elegantly choreographed by Casey Nicholaw. Well . . . that was the idea.

Instead, I went to open the door, and *off* came the doorknob. No door, just a doorknob in my hand. Amazing how time slows when under duress. Staring at that open hole in the door where there had just been a doorknob seemed like an eternity . . . "What to do? *Oh*! I know!!" I marched up to the next leg, leading to the wings, thinking, "I'll go open it from the other side. . . ." Brilliant. Except for the set piece waiting there to come on . . . on a pallet . . . in pitch black. *Splat*. Down I went onto all fours. Ow. But the cast was still waiting . . . waiting . . . *waiting* . . . scratching at the door . . . until I was able to limp over there and open it. At last!

Ah yes, hey-ho for the glamorous life of a Swing!

TRIPP HANSON (The Drowsy Chaperone,
Kiss Me Kate, Boys from Syracuse)

Justin Greer

Shrek the Musical was a unique experience in so many ways, not the least of which being that our Swings each had their own specific fairy tale creature costume. I was a Wizard . . . a big, fabulous Wizard who is *very* gay, loves Cole Porter musicals, and is obsessed with Liza Minnelli. My character's nickname is the Gizard (for Gay Wizard) or Wizard with a Z. He's very grand, and has an *amazing* costume, with big hair, a big prosthetic nose, and a crown of sticks that will poke your eye out, if you aren't careful.

Since the regular cast fairy tale creatures had very specific material to perform, their material oftentimes needed to be adjusted when a Swing went on in the Swing costume. Further complicating matters was the fact that we had two female Swings covering eight women, but we often had more than two women out of the show. As the Dance Captain, I became the de facto third female Swing.

One time, the Gizard was on for the Shoemaker's Elf, usually played by Jen Cody. I usually did my utmost to sing in the proper range of the people I was replacing, and the first time I was on for the Elf, I didn't give much thought to the range of her solo singing. This was a mistake. She had a line that was very featured, which was "It's time I told the world I'm a Scientologist!" The entire Ensemble then echoed the word "Scientologist" as a celebration of her bravery in revealing this secret. When the Gizard came downstage center to proclaim this information in a truly committed way, I realized halfway through the line that I wasn't going to make the ending notes. So in order to get the joke across, I decided to speak-sing the part that was high for me. This came out as a cross between "Monster Mash" and Paul Lynde in his center square. To say the Ensemble echo of "Scientologist" was anemic would be an understatement.

[Another time] I was sitting in the back of the house watching a performance of *Anything Goes* [where I was a Swing] when someone runs to tell me to get backstage. I know it isn't good, so as I am running I begin taking off my clothes. Along the way I find out that Josh Franklin ran into Anthony Wayne Johnson and was bleeding (not a great thing, particularly for a show where all the sailors wear white). I get down to the dressing room and see Josh bleeding, throw my costume on, and run to the stage just in time to make Josh's entrance for "Buddy Beware," a number with Erma and the sailors involving lifts and throws. I get onstage and realize that Anthony isn't there. I begin to calculate what needs to be done to ensure Jess Stone's safety, since she is currently singing her number with five sailors and not six.

Meanwhile, the other male Swing, Mark Ledbetter, was about to leave the building when he saw Anthony covered in blood. Mark rushed to the dressing room to see *me* getting ready to go on, thinking that I was going on for Anthony. Mark didn't notice Josh bleeding in the corner of the dressing room until after I had left. Mark then realized what had happened, quickly got into his costume, and managed to enter into the number at the perfect moment so that no one in the audience would have ever realized that anything was wrong. To this day, that is the most harrowing and extraordinary Swing save of which I have been a part.

JUSTIN GREER (*Anything Goes, The Mystery of Edwin Drood, Shrek, The Producers*)

Kristine Bendul

I was not a Swing or cover in *Movin' Out*, but I ended up having an incredible Swing moment regardless. I usually danced the Mulberry Street feature with "Tony" onstage right while "Brenda" danced with three men onstage left, executing a series of lift after lift. One show, Keith Roberts kept looking over his shoulder more than usual and I thought, "Wow, his character is really into 'Brenda' tonight." Little did I know but "Brenda" never made it onstage due to a shoulder injury in the previous number. All I know is Keith grabbed me by my shoulders and asked me, "Do you know it?!" I said yes and the next thing I know, he shoves me, with love, to stage left into the arms of the three men just as the lift sequence began. That gave the understudy enough time to get ready and I ended up with another incredible experience that would only happen in live theatre!

KRISTINE BENDUL (*Come Fly Away,*
Man of La Mancha, Swing!)

Brad Bradley

After six Broadway shows and witnessing the amount of work that Swings do, I swore I would never do it. I will fully acknowledge that Swings are the hardest working folks in Show Biz and I wanted none of it. I also have to admit that phrases like "Swing option" [getting to leave before the show is done] used to piss me off, and watching them wave from the wings as they exit the theatre thirty minutes before curtain call used to drive me crazy. I used to resent that it looked like they got paid to just sit there and watch movies.

The circumstances seemed to fall into place: My contract was ending with *Billy Elliot* and I heard about a new show called *People in the Picture* that was still looking for a male Swing. The Choreographer was Andy Blankenbuehler, who I was in the Ensemble of *Steel Pier* with. The project was original and was source material, which is unheard of these days. The show was a limited run. These several things piqued my interest, but [there] also was the fact I would only cover four men, two dancer singers, and two Actor dancers. All of these factors, plus the fact I didn't have to audition, led the "I'll never swing" to signing on the dotted line.

This [job] was harder on my ego than I would have imagined. I had made a good career as a Broadway Understudy up to this point, and figured it would be similar. It's not at all. In those cases, I was also in the show and had my own track to focus on and create, plus another Principal role. This was overwhelming and frustrating. I was cut out for this job talent wise, but not emotionally or spiritually. I realize I had it easy too, only four tracks. I've seen guys with eight (possibly twelve if they had to) in *Billy Elliot*, with second covers. Granted, all four tracks had little in common and there was no unison dancing, which made it harder. All my Actors had distinct characters and journeys, which is why I said yes in the first place.

Opening came and my mom flew in from California and it still had the excitement of a new Broadway show opening; Gypsy Robe, flowers, gifts, hugs. The big exception was that at half-hour I felt invisible. I went out into the audience to experience what it felt like to be in the house on an Opening Night. It was exciting to see people dressed up, and walk my Mom to her seat, but I wanted to be getting into a costume more than anything, and this was night one. There was no "good job" at the party, but then again, when you are in the Ensemble of a Broadway show there is rarely "good job" said at any party.

The first time I went on was for a non-dancing track and the part I most wanted to go on for. I had three intimate scenes with Donna Murphy. (She had flowers sent to me to wish me luck.) It was so special and she was so present for me. My take on the character was completely different and she went right along with me. I felt confident with my choices and proud of the work. Yes, there were things that went wrong, but most of them were platform moves, set changes, spike marks [taped markings on the stage, denoting placement of set pieces], and things you can't know until you are actually onstage.

I began to understand the life of a Swing much more as the run progressed, and yes, I had my backpack on well before curtain call and was out the door just like those I resented in the past. I realized it wasn't out of disrespect; it was because I was no longer needed. I did begin to work on other projects during the show, but never actually watched a movie. If we had run longer, I'm sure I would have.

Despite all the disappointments with the show, I do not regret the opportunity and take away only great pride with the accomplishment.

The experience ended with a bad taste in my mouth. It was decided that a cast album would be done and the Swings and Stand-bys would not be included. This was something I wanted to avoid from contract-signing day, but was inevitable. The kicker really was that the Stand-bys wouldn't be on it anyway because they did not sing the Ensemble stuff; the other Swing/Dance Captain had left the show, so honestly it was just me that wasn't asked. I begged and pleaded, asked to do it for free, and they said no. They informed me that legally since I am an original cast member my name has to be on the album, so everyone would think I was on it. Needless to say I left closing night at my Swing option departure, skipped the party, and went straight to Fire Island. Until writing this, I tried not to think about the experience. (Okay that's a lie, I think about doing scene work with Donna Murphy all the time.)

BRAD BRADLEY (The People in the Picture)

Colin Bradbury

One time in *A Chorus Line*, one of our understudies was on for Richie and hurt his rib during the opening number. He finished the combination and collapsed offstage. Once we realized he was seriously injured and couldn't finish the show, we had to whisper to people onstage to tell the other Understudy (in the Ensemble) that he would have to finish the show as Richie. That particular Actor was playing his normal role as ("Wrong Arms") Roy, the Cut Dancer who dances less than adequately and gets cut because he can't get the arms right. Roy is normally cut after the opening number, but this one performance he had to stay in his Roy costume but finish the show playing Richie. At the end of the show, Richie is hired for the show that they've all been auditioning for. So it was possibly the first time in history that Roy was technically hired for the show! And what's amazing is that two Actors came offstage part way through the show and had *no* idea that someone else was playing Richie in the wrong costume. That's how much some people [neglect to] notice what is going on around them, unlike a Swing who has to be extra aware of their surroundings.

COLIN BRADBURY (*Come Fly Away, The Book of Mormon*— First National Tour, *A Chorus Line*—First National Tour)

Clinton Roane

I went to lunch with a friend, who is also a Swing in an off-Broadway show, and I was telling him that I [would] *never* go on anytime soon. As he walked me to my theatre he jokingly said, "Have a great show!!" I rolled my eyes, signed in, and went to my Swing dressing room. My pre-show ritual normally starts with me arriving to the theatre at least an hour and a half before the call time . . . but not that day. I got there right at 2:30 (our show started at 3:00). When I signed in, I noticed that two of the people I covered hadn't signed in. I didn't think much of it though because their dressing rooms were open and people forget to sign in all the time. As time went on, and got closer to show time, only one of them had showed up. The other guy (for whom I was the first cover) still hadn't arrived. Something in my head said "Read over your notes Clinton . . . *now!*" I read a few, then got antsy and checked the sign-in sheet again . . . he still hadn't showed up. At this point I was freaking out. I went to the Stage Manager's office, told the Assistant Stage Manager that so-and-so hadn't signed in and a look of panic came across her face. As she ran to check the Call Board, I ran to read over some more notes and charts. Before I could flip two pages, the Stage Manager got on the intercom and said "*Aaaaand* we have a cast change! At this performance the role of Willie Roberson will be played by Clinton Roane!" There were cheers on my floor of the theatre, but panic in my eyes!! My other Swings asked me if I was ready, people started to swarm me making sure I knew everything I needed to know . . . and suddenly my mind went blank. All I could think about were those chairs and some of the transitions were slipping from my memory 'cause I was *so* overwhelmed. Before I could try and get a word out, the Stage Manager announced, "Clinton please run to Wardrobe *now.*" I was quickly thrown into that Actor's costume and mic because I didn't have one yet. Jeff [Whiting], Stroman's Associate, was there to help me through everything. He asked if I needed anything and I said "Call my mom."

Before I knew it, I was in the pre-show circle and next on the stage . . . with lights . . . costume . . . an audience . . . and my cast members. They really helped me get through the show. Some would secretly point out where I should go. Some literally threw me there. Before I knew it, the show was over and I had *just* made my Broadway debut. It all happened so fast. But I know that the preparation I had is what ultimately led to me having the confidence to go on that stage and do what I was paid to do . . . be a Swing!

CLINTON ROANE (*The Scottsboro Boys*)

Brian Collier

I was on the Swing/Dance Captain committee for Actors' Equity Association when [Production Contract] negotiations came up. We put together a huge presentation for the League producers. I was floored, after talking to some of them, that they had no idea what we actually did. So I pulled out a cast cut-sheet and Tracking Sheet for a show earlier in the week. It had thirteen people out, with six Swings to cover, and spanned three pages. I color-coded it so that the producers could see how much internal bouncing around each person had to do. We got our raise.

BRIAN COLLIER (*Mary Poppins, Cats*—National Tour)

Alicia Albright

In *Wicked* there are these characters called the "Flatheads," they are large weeble-wobble-like characters that are a reference to the novel *Wicked*. When we wear the costume we have literal clown shoes that are twice the size of our own feet, so you always have to walk, jump, or march heel-toe or you will fall over. On top of that . . . you are inside and strapped into a huge egg, in which you can't use your arms because they are in the belly of the costume. And you have to control a pole that pops the head up and down and you can only see through tiny holes in the chin of the "flathead's" head.

So one day I was on for the onstage Swing track. (Our onstage Swings are only in four or five numbers in the show but are already mic-ed and ready to go should anyone go down mid show.) So this particular onstage track happens to perform the center flathead—a very prestigious position. And in this flathead position you can underdress your own clothing because you can't see it through the costume. So, like I said, I was on for this track this particular day and happened to be wearing my favorite bright, *bright* pink jacket. Anyway, I go to get ready and as I am standing with my Dresser we realize we have the wrong pants/lower half for my particular flathead upper body! They completely zip around your whole body to attach the pants to the top part and if it isn't the right pants the zipper won't line up. So my Dresser and I decide the show must go on and she safety pins the pants to the top . . . which wasn't the best idea because the pants are very heavy. And I keep thinking "oh no, this could go terribly wrong" and just as I finish that thought my entrance music starts and I decide to just go for it.

I bounce onto stage (because the more you bounce and the higher your knees are, the better it looks) holding the pole that tries to bash you in the face with one hand, and holding up the pants with the other. As I am bouncing out, I feel the safety pins pop, pop, popping open so I just keep clutching the front as hard as I can . . . until . . . I have to pop the head up and I have to use both hands to do that and as I did my pants fell down to my ankles . . . on center stage . . . on Broadway . . . annnddd . . . exposing my favorite bright pink jacket in all its glory!!! *Aaaaaaahhh*!! The whole cast and [the] audience starts to laugh as I frantically try to pull my pants up, which are now caught on the wrong side of the head pole so I can't get them up and you just see bright pink elbows flapping up and down as I frantically keep trying to pull them up! I finally get them a little up and finally shuffle offstage . . . absolutely mortified but laughing because what else can you do in that situation.

To this day, my Stage Manager tells me it's the worst thing she's ever seen on Broadway, and she has seen a lot. I just have to laugh it off and know that I am now famous in the world of *Wicked* for onstage mishaps, and I wear it like a badge of honor. The beautiful thing about live theatre and swinging especially is that absolutely anything can happen, and that is what makes it so great!

ALICIA ALBRIGHT (*Wicked*—Universal Swing,
All Shook Up—First National Tour, *A Chorus Line*—
Hawaiian Tour and TUTS Houston)

Romain Frugé

In 1993, I was a Swing in the original cast of *The Who's Tommy*, covering all the young guys including Cousin Kevin and Tommy. The first preview was a Tuesday evening and Anthony Barrile, playing Cousin Kevin, who had been having vocal troubles, felt increasingly worse as the performance went on. He made it through the show but felt there was no way he'd be able to go on for the next performance, a Wednesday matinee. I was up. I was getting thrown on in a major role on Broadway with basically no rehearsal!

I went home to my East Village apartment that night and remember very clearly staring at the ceiling and thinking, "I could just get on a bus and leave New York and never come back." I lay awake all night.

The next morning, exhausted, I got in a cab to go up to the theatre for an emergency rehearsal called for 10:00 a.m. and I remember a sort of peace washing over me, "Well, it's not brain surgery. No one's life is at stake." I met the Stage Managers and Assistant Directors in an upstairs lobby to go over music and talk through the Cousin Kevin track. Then I remember walking down the aisle of the theatre, the cast, called in early, sitting in the orchestra seats watching me with looks of trepidation and empathy.

We marked through the big production numbers in hopes of averting major train wrecks and then the next thing I remember I was standing stage left, dressed as Kevin, toy airplane in hand, and as the opening hammer blows from the overture were playing and my entrance approached I thought, "Just jump off the cliff." And I did.

I don't remember much about the performance. It passed by in a kind of dream but it went well, I think, mostly due to the great Stage Management team who dragged me around backstage from one entrance to the next—across, up, and under the stage through the complex moving maze of spinning sets, trapdoors, and dancing people.

Then it was over. Pete Townshend himself came up to my dressing room shaking his head and in his beautiful west London accent said, "I don't know how you did that!" Then he pulled a hundred dollar bill from his wallet and gave it to me. A tip, I guess. I don't know—but an unforgettable moment in a day I'll never forget!

ROMAIN FRUGÉ (*Titanic, The Who's Tommy, The Secret Garden, Big River*)

Stacey Lynn Brass

In February of 1978 when I was ten years old, I was hired as the Swing for five orphans in the Broadway Company of *Annie*. The Swing position was to cover all of the orphans except Annie and Molly (the littlest orphan), who were covered by other orphans in the show. I was hired on a Friday afternoon and my contract started the following Tuesday. On Tuesday I showed up at 10:00 a.m. for rehearsal all day with the Dance Captain and Stage Manager who were teaching me the show and, beginning that night, I sat on a stool in the back of the orchestra next to the lighting booth and watched the show. Technically, I was already the Swing. So, even though I was rehearsing during the day, I had to be at the theatre for every performance.

At this time, Sarah Jessica Parker was playing Annie. On the first Saturday of my first week, after I had rehearsed for three days and had watched five performances, I was sitting on my stool watching the Saturday matinee and during "Hard Knock Life" Sarah went running off of the stage. I watched as the orphan who was the Annie understudy (Duffy) started "playing" Annie mid-song, and how all of the orphans just adjusted and finished the number and subsequent scene. At the end of the scene, which was right before the "Tomorrow" scene, the curtain came down and the house lights came up. I jumped off of my stool and ran over to the stage mothers that were all standing along the rail behind the last row and tugged a pant leg and asked what was going on. One of them said to me "You better go sit on your stool so that they know where to find you!" Two minutes later the Stage Manager came out to get me and whisked me backstage and up to the orphan's dressing room where someone started putting me in a costume, someone else started making my messy pigtails, and the Dance Captain was sitting in front of me with the "bible" reviewing what I had learned that week. I remember her saying to me, "So do you remember what you learned this week? You go here, and then here . . ."

They had already changed the Annie understudy into her wig and costume, the curtain was up, and I could hear her singing "Tomorrow" over the loud speakers. The orphans were going on in two scenes. Five minutes later I was in the wing stage right lined up to walk on behind Miss Hannigan for the "Little Girls" scene. I was on as Pepper and it was an epic moment of my life.

At intermission, I went down to the payphone in the basement across from the women's chorus dressing room and made a collect call to my parents to tell them that I was in fact making my Broadway debut. When my mom didn't answer the phone at home I called my dad at work. When my father came to the phone I said "Hi daddy, I'm on!" and he said "What?" as if he *had* to have heard me wrong and so I said "I'm in the show!" I will never forget the sound of his voice as I heard my dad make a crying sound and say to whoever was standing there "My daughter's on Broadway and I'm not there to see it!"

Sarah Jessica Parker had in fact broken her tooth that afternoon with her wooden scrub brush during "Hard Knock Life." After being rushed to a dentist for emergency treatment, she was back by

7:30 p.m. and ready to go on that night. As luck would have it, even though my parents got in the car immediately and drove in hoping I would be on again that night, they did not get to see me perform that day. But they did many more times as I went on to become the permanent Swing and then eventually one of the orphans. I was with the *Annie* Company for two years and wouldn't trade one minute of it!

STACEY LYNN BRASS (*Annie*)

Larry Fuller

I was [the Jet] Swing on the original *West Side Story*. I was hired the first week they were open, so my name is not in the Opening Night program credits. At that time, Equity allowed a cast member to do a partial show, so I would dance for everyone except Tony and Riff. The Actor would do their scenes and songs and when the dancing started, he would slip offstage and I would slip on and dance in his place. After the number during applause, he would slip back on and I would slip off. Well it was really bad for the Understudy because then A-Rab and Baby John and Action and Diesel and whoever could [say], "Oh, I don't feel well today," or "I turned my ankle so I can do everything but I can't dance," and the Understudy didn't get to go on—they'd put me on.

While I was the Jet Swing in the original *West Side Story*, the Dance Captain, Howard Jeffery, would also put me on for a Shark now and then. Howard was supposed to be the Shark Swing, but he didn't like to go on. One night during a flu epidemic there were several people out from both gangs, so even with Howard on, I also had to fill in for about three Jets and two Sharks. I had two Dressers with me all the time. Every time I came off they would change my costume and complexion. My skin color would be light in one scene and dark in another, according to the costume of the gang I was part of. It was confusing but we pulled it off.

The first time I was in and Jerry [Jerome Robbins] came to see the show we were told to get back to the stage ASAP after the show because Jerry was going to be giving notes. So I got to the stage before anyone else so I could be close to "God." Jerry gave notes for about forty-five minutes without ever looking at me. Since he hadn't said anything to me, at the end I was thinking, I guess I was okay. Then the very last note was when he turned to me, held up his thumb, and said, "You stuck out like that with a sore on it." That's all he said and the note session was over. Well, I thought I was fired. I certainly was very humiliated, being the only new member of the Company at that point. Luckily, two of my fellow cast members came to me and said they wanted to take me out for a beer. Their names are Tony Mordente and Jay Norman. They must have seen how miserable and in shock I was. So we went to the corner bar and they told me every member of that cast had been through what I had just been through, most of them more than once. That the cast had great respect for my work in the show, but that maybe I should stop worrying so much about the steps and positions and start thinking about being a Jet more. So that's what I did and it was one of the best lessons of my early career. I was only nineteen then.

LARRY FULLER (Choreographer of Seven Broadway shows; Swing on *Funny Girl, West Side Story*)

Jerome Vivona

[In] *Jerome Robbins' Broadway* I covered a combination of over 130 tracks in that show: male and female. And often, many tracks [were] "blended" [combining multiple tracks into one]. It was not uncommon for me to be onstage performing one Jet track and look over into the wing where George Russell and Cynthia Onrubia (Dance Captains) would be standing holding a vest or Jet jacket symbolizing my transition into a different track that I would assume from that point on while still fulfilling the requirements of the current role. It was an on-the-fly assessment of what was required and an immediate adjustment in the hopes of making a seamless transition for the onstage cast and myself. It was thrilling and remarkably rewarding to succeed under those circumstances.

JEROME VIVONA (*Thoroughly Modern Millie, Gypsy, Anything Goes, Sweet Charity*)

Joseph Medeiros

I was a Swing when I was eleven years old for *Big the Musical*. I went on in the middle of the show and I totally blew it. It was horrible. Part of it was because I wasn't prepared and I kind of felt like I was not part of the show and I was like, "Oh, I know it, it's fine." I totally blew it, my first night on [Broadway]. And everybody knew it and I was really upset afterwards. I spoke with Susan Stroman actually. The next day at rehearsal I went up and apologized. She was very, very sweet but it was clear, "We saw you do well before [during the out-of-town tryout], which is why you're still here, and everything's fine, but you have to do your job"—which is a tough conversation for an 11-year-old to have. So, I never messed up again. You know, that is something that has stayed with me since then. I feel like a different person—just the idea of always being prepared. I learned that lesson. You have to be ready. And I've had experiences, since then, where I've been asked to learn something immediately, and go on and do it. Like in summer stock, where there are no understudies, and you're doing *Cats*, and someone gets hurt, and after the show they go, "Could you come in and maybe learn Mungojerrie tomorrow afternoon and do it for the rest of the run?" And I say, "Oh yeah, sure, sure." And that is one of the most exciting things—knowing if something goes wrong and they need somebody to just do it, I can do that.

JOSEPH MEDEIROS (*West Side Story*, *Big*)

Karen Hyland

I was one of four Swings of *Ghost the Musical*—two boys (one of which was a Dance Captain) and two girls. We were in Previews, and our Dance Captain was on for the first time, as well as the other male Swing. The other female Swing, the Choreographer, and I were watching the show from the back of the house. It was the middle of Act Two, and our Dance Captain did a tumbling pass in one of the numbers and immediately ran off the stage. We all put our hands over our mouths in shock. He looked really hurt. But everyone just stood there.

I knew that the final dance number of the show was (
and the entire number was about moving luggage trunk
female lead walked on. No one could be missing from tha   ..ber.
However our other male Swing was already on! I ran backstage
and our Dance Captain was clutching his ankle, and said his
Achilles had snapped. I ran back around, got the Choreographer,
and told him to come back because he was really hurt. On the way,
I said, "I'll do the track for 'I'm Outta Here.'" The Choreographer
seemed iffy about it, but there was no time. I said, even if I looked
ridiculous, I would know where to move the trunks. Before anyone
could entirely object I was in full wig prep and costume. I didn't
even have time to panic. I just did it.

There was a lot of improv dancing around the stage, and I'm
sure during those parts I just looked for my trunks, and where they
needed to go. But the [trunks] all got there!

KAREN HYLAND (*Scandalous, Ghost,*
Billy Elliot—Second National Tour)

Katrina Yaukey

In the 2006 revival of *Company*, a week and a half after opening,
one of the girls came down with laryngitis. I got a call on a Tuesday,
probably two hours before the show, that I was going to do her
track. I had watched the show but never walked through the show
onstage and I'd only sung her song once before in a rehearsal.
Anyway, I get to the theatre, and I'm on for, what ended up being, a
week. When she finally returned on a matinee day, after that week,
not only had she been dealing with laryngitis, she'd also had pinkeye.

As Swings in *Company*, we would come in and practice our
instruments and play along with the show. On the matinee when
she came back into the show, I am in a baseball hat and jeans, and
I'm practicing the saxophone, during the show, in our Swing room
backstage. I hear something in the hallway, over the monitor, and
I say to the other Swings, "You know what guys, maybe we should
go check, we did turn the monitors down." So, I'm walking, with
my saxophone, down the steps from our fifth floor practice area,
and I see Raul Esparza's Dresser coming upstairs, "You're on!"

The song I'm supposed to sing is in two and a half minutes. I run down the stairs, get to Stage Management, and the girl I'm covering is on the floor coughing over a bucket. She has left the stage. This doesn't happen in a John Doyle show, you don't leave the stage for the entire show, except intermission. Stage Management says, "Go downstairs, get ready as quickly as you can, she's going to try to start the song."

There are three sections to the song, with a scene in between each one. I finish getting ready and come up the stairs to stand by, next to the Stage Manager calling the show. During the second section, we could see her looking over to see if I'm going to make an entrance. However, since she'd had pink eye, she couldn't quite see if I was there. She's standing by the piano singing, "... and another hundred people just got off of the train ... " and she's singing it, well, speaking it really, because she's having a lot of trouble. During the second scene where she has a moment not singing, I walk onstage, and she can see me, as I get a few feet away from her. She hops off the piano, we cross, I turn into place and sing, "... and another hundred people ..." it was like a two-second change. You could see Raul [Esparza] who was facing downstage tilt his head in a sort of "Huh?" I mean [we have] completely different voices. And the audience was like, "Uhhhhhhh," and afterwards there was a pause, and it was kind of awkward. We could not have been more different. But that's my all-time craziest story—going on mid-song.

KATRINA YAUKEY (*Company*, *Cabaret 1998*,
Billy Elliot, *Warhorse*, *Cabaret 2014*)

Lucy Costelloe

In *Dirty Dancing* I was Dance Captain, Swing, and cover Mrs. Schuhmacher. In one particular Cut-Show I had to spring from playing Mrs. Schuhmacher in one scene, to playing Ensemble in another, then back again, etc. Mrs. Schuhmacher is the little old lady, and I had heavy makeup and a wig because I was only in my twenties, actually. So, the Cut-Show meant some very stressy costume, wig, and makeup changes. Everything had gone well, I'd made all the changes, and we were right near the end, just doing our choreographed bows. In this number I was in the Ensemble role, dancing an energetic jive with lots of lifts with my partner in the spotlight, and the audience was going wild, standing and cheering. At first I thought I must have danced really well to get this kind of reaction, but then I realized I still had my old lady wig on. The audience thought it was a real old lady being thrown around the boy's head and being plunged into backbends, so they were really impressed! When I came back onstage a few minutes later for my bow as Mrs. Schuhmacher, I got the biggest cheer of my career!

LUCY COSTELLOE (*Tanz der Vampire*—Germany, *Dirty Dancing*—Germany, *Singing In The Rain*—UK)

Ben Hartley

I do have one story which I am slightly ashamed of. I will preface this story by saying in my youth I was a curious little bugger. During my time at *Cats* in the West End, we were getting close to the Opening Night for the cast change I was part of. During a stage rehearsal of one of the women's numbers, I thought it would be a good idea to go and familiarize myself with the underground tunnels that led out to the audience. As this was the original set for *Cats*, it was quite the maze to figure out.

Feeling tenacious, I took my Swing bible backstage and climbed down into the area of the tunnel entrances. As I started to mark which character used which tunnel and where that led to, I ventured further underneath the stage as there were other tunnels to see. I came into a clearing and suddenly found a toilet placed on the ground. It was a slightly strange thing to see because it wasn't attached to anything but had a chain rope above it. Now for everyone in the US, old English pubs and toilets for the most part back in the day had these types of chains that you would pull to flush the toilet. So I looked into the bowl, I checked around the back, I looked at the chain, and I pulled.

Big mistake! I instantly heard screams from the stage above and then fits of laughter. I thought for a second that I had killed someone, or set off the trap door. I thought my life was over as I knew it and I was surely going to get fired on the spot. What to do, think quick, think quick. . . . As the Stage Management quickly ran underneath the stage to find me sat on the toilet with my head in my hands smiling the biggest innocent smile I have ever conjured up, I told a small white lie that I had tripped and fallen and accidentally grabbed the chain to catch myself obviously setting something off. I told them about checking out the tunnels but none of this impressed anyone.

I don't think they believed my short story, but the most important part is that I set off the Mr. Mistoffelees can trick. In the middle of his solo he magically makes a can jump out of the floor and ribbons fly everywhere. The can had hit the Musical Director in the back and sent him flying into the cast wrapping ribbons around his entire body. He basically looked like rainbow-colored road kill or a mummy at the Gay Pride festival.

Needless to say, I sat down and did as I was told for the rest of the rehearsal and didn't move a muscle. Note to self, don't go discovering in places you don't belong and tenacity will only get you so far. I have since become less curious after this "chain" of events.

BEN HARTLEY (*Enron*, *Cats*—UK)

Candi Boyd

I was with the Broadway Company [of *Jersey Boys*]. One Saturday in the Fall of 2012, I wasn't onstage but I was backstage swinging. I got this urgent call from our production company during the Second Act that one of the actresses on the tour had completely lost her voice and another was at a wedding. Could I be there, in New Haven, Connecticut, by half-hour of their night show, 7:30 p.m., with all my costumes and wigs?!

We made it happen! I left the matinee in a black car to Brooklyn to pack an overnight bag, while the car waited and drove me back ($100). When I got back, the tour's Company Manager had sped the whole way from New Haven, in her rental [car], and they were packing my costumes and wigs into her car. We drove more than a little over the speed limit, while I did my makeup and we arrived at the theatre in New Haven at 7:22 p.m., where all my wigs and costumes were snatched, I grabbed a coffee, took a quick tour of backstage and did a flawless performance! Two shows in two states in one day!

CANDI BOYD (Jersey Boys—Universal Swing)

Michael Biren

My favorite story is from *Billy Elliot* when I went on for Mr. Braithwaite with an hour's notice [which I didn't cover at the time]. We were in LA and were having a lot of trouble with our Braithwaite covers. They were all nursing injuries. I got a call from our Stage Manager, about an hour and a half before half-hour, telling me that the guy playing Braithwaite and both understudies had called out. I believe the exact sentence went like this, ". . . and I believe, unless I'm mistaken, that you are next." He got off the phone, re-called all three to make sure they couldn't do the show, and then called me back to tell me I was on. I was at a farmer's market that was really close to the theatre. I ran to the theatre, met the Resident Choreographer, the Resident Director, our Wardrobe people, Musical Director, and Stage Manager. I had to have costumes fit on to me, a wig (that almost fell off during the first performance), and had to learn a tap dance with a jump rope as well as a dance solo, and because most of the automation in the show was cut, that part had become responsible for a ton of set moves. There was so much adrenaline pumping through my body. Both shows went great but I was on the edge of my seat the entire time. That part got his own bow in the finale and the cast was so incredibly supportive and stopped choreography to clap for me, it was amazing. After the second show, I went back to this house we were renting in the Hollywood Hills, sat in the hot tub with a beer, and looked over the city. It was an incredible feeling. There are moments in your life as a Swing when you can really say "I did my job today," and that was definitely one of them . . . I take it back, that was the best I have ever slept.

MICHAEL BIREN (Billy Elliot—Second National Tour,
A Funny Thing Happened . . .—Goodspeed)

12

Thoughts from the Creative Team

Questions and Answers with Susan Stroman, Jerry Mitchell, and Rob Ashford

Susan Stroman

When did you first discover the value of a Swing?

I would say it wasn't until I did *The World Goes 'Round*, which is a show I created Off Broadway with Scott Ellis and David Thompson. Finding Swings for that show was not an easy task. There are only five characters, but they all have to dance *and* roller-skate *and* sing. And, of course, there was only enough money for one male and one female. Between what the music department needed vocally and what I needed physically—finding one guy and one gal to fit the bill was tough. *Crazy for You* presented the same challenge. That show has a huge amount of Choreography, and finding someone who could hold the stage as a Principal and also do those steps was incredibly difficult. So it was early in my career, right around the time I started choreographing and directing, when I recognized how important Swings are. And I think Swings are even more important now, because when I first started there weren't any personal days or outs or vacations. You had to put a gun to someone's head to make him miss a show. Today the Swings are as important as your Principals—not only do they keep the curtain up when an Actor is out, but if it's a lead role they're covering, they have to make the audience feel as if it hasn't missed a thing.

Do you think there is a natural progression Swings seem to make (from Swing to Dance Captain to Associate to Choreographer)?

To be a really good Swing you have to have an incredible mind. I delight in watching Swings do what they do—how they can cover ten tracks and go on for Principals, too. So naturally they make great Dance Captains and Associates—if that's the path they want to take. When I'm creating a new piece, I always want the Swings with me in **Pre-Production**. I want them to understand the subtext of why something was created in a particular way and to know where the ideas and motivation have come from. Absorbing all of that is what makes them so valuable, because not only will they be maintaining the show, but very possibly they will be recreating it all over the world. I've been very fortunate to have a lot of my shows go on National Tours and to open internationally in London or Tokyo, and it's the Swings who help remount those productions. For example, Joanne Manning was a Swing in the Broadway Company of *Contact*. She and the show's Dance Captain, Scott Taylor, were responsible for mounting productions of *Contact* in London and for Shiki Theatre Company in Japan. Scott has actually swung for me on many shows, including *Crazy for You*, and also helped recreate *Show Boat* in London. Nothing thrills me more than when someone who loves to swing seizes an opportunity to make more of it and really does it. Whether that means moving into an Associate position, maintaining a show, remounting a show—it's just a really fantastic moment.

What misconceptions do you think people have about the role of a Swing?

If I see a young Actor being disrespectful towards a Swing, it's usually because he doesn't understand what a Swing really does. Actors are constantly being pulled out of rehearsal for costume fittings, and when that happens, a Swing will step in. I've found there are usually one or two dancers who have some secret thing you don't know about—how to travel from one side of the room to the other to make a cue, or maybe a special way of partnering, or where to pick up a prop. So I make a point of always telling the Company, "Respect your Swings. They are going to be the heroes of this production, so take time with them to work out whatever it is you need to work out. Any information you need to share, share it with the Swings." And once you move into the theatre, those of us out front have no way of knowing that the only way you're making it onstage is by leaping over a hay wagon. That's the kind of essential information you must share with a Swing because he or she often has no way of knowing unless you tell them. Of course, it's nice to have someone who maintains the show, like Tara Young or Chris Peterson, be on hand to help communicate. But I think probably the biggest misconception younger Actors have is that someone is a Swing because he or she wasn't good enough to be in one of the Ensemble roles. And that's completely wrong—at least in my world it is. I cast a Swing because I already know he's very smart, or I can tell in an audition that she's intelligent. I don't take the Swing position lightly.

What do you look for in auditions, when casting a Swing?

I clock how quickly someone picks up the steps during an audition. I'll often ask that dancer to do the combination again, except dance it as if she's shy, or hostile, or drunk, or flirtatious. I'm watching to see how someone takes direction and if you do that well and you're quick, then I'll most likely consider you for a Swing position. I can see it immediately.

How do you decide how many Swings you are going to hire for a show?

I always want more Swings, however that's not always my choice to make—usually the budget decides for you. Of course every show is different, so it often depends on what you need covered. In *The Scottsboro Boys* there are twelve male roles that range from quite young to quite old and we managed with three male Swings. We had an older Swing, J.C. Montgomery, to cover the Interlocutor as well as Tambo and Bones. And because some of the Scottsboro Boys were as young as thirteen, we had a younger Swing, Clinton Roane, who could play that age range. And we had E. Clayton Cornelious, who is a little older than Clinton, who could cover the 19-year-olds and the 20-year-olds. However, we also have a lady—*the* Lady—and in order to have a cover for her and for it to be cost effective, our Producer was able to hire her on an Equity contract that allowed her to swing but also to be an Assistant Stage Manager. So really it's finances and the range of characters that will determine the number of Swings.

How do you convince Producers to hire more Swings than they might think are necessary?

You have to lay it out and explain that the show can't go on if we aren't covered properly. To use *The Scottsboro Boys* again as an example, the show can't go on if you only have eight Actors because historically there were nine Scottsboro Boys. It wouldn't make sense to continue. In *Contact* you need someone strong enough to do the acrobatics on the swing, you need someone sexy enough to play The Girl in the Yellow Dress, and you need someone who can really act to play The Wife. Those are three very different roles that require three very different dancers.

How do you deal with specialty elements (e.g., aerial work) in your shows, like The Frogs, and how do you help your Swings to stay in shape and learn these skills?

With any specialty, like aerial silks, I first ask the Actors if this is something they're willing to do. In *The Frogs*, I knew that would be a whole new skill for them, something that would change their bodies and give them strength, but I also knew it could be dangerous. I couldn't simply say to the girls, "Let's just try this!" So I asked them if they were up for it—and they were. The Swings were included in that conversation, and they learned to master the silks right alongside the other girls. The producers allowed us to hang the silks in the lobby of the Vivian Beaumont and every day during rehearsal we had class. And the Swings had to be part of that process. Another example is *The Music Man*—I was curious about what happened to the people of River City after the show ends. I imagined they would be playing instruments that Harold Hill had given them, so I thought it would be fun if they all played the trombone during the curtain call. I asked the Producers if I could have trombone lessons for the cast every day at four o'clock during rehearsal. I thought either this will work or it won't, but it's worth taking a chance because it could be incredible. Of course the Swings are there too, learning to play the trombone because if they have to go on for someone then they'll have to play the trombone too. But more importantly, they have to experience learning to play the trombone, to tap into the pride of having accomplished something great. They have to be part of that because it's essential to these characters and our story.

How do you help your new Swings to take on this complicated job, especially if they are younger?

On the first day, you have to pull the Swings aside, especially the little ones, and explain to them how to write it down and how to take it in and where to sit and where to watch. I always have a table in the rehearsal room that is devoted to the Swings. And during Tech, the Swings have their own table in the house and no one else can sit there. That tells the Company how important I think the Swings are and encourages them to treat them with respect. You have to set it up that way, by first making sure the Swings understand what their job is and then by making sure the Company understands how important the Swings are and how to communicate with each other. You have to help people understand their job, and give them every opportunity to get something right.

What are your expectations of a Swing in rehearsal?

When I'm teaching something new to a Principal, I'll tell the Swing to just watch the first time through. I want that Principal Actor to feel like he's creating the steps or the movement—that it's coming from him. The next time we rehearse, I'll tell the Swing to shadow it in the back. After that, it's absolutely fine to get up in rehearsal and do it. If we're doing a run through it's probably better to sit and watch, but when I'm breaking down a scene in rehearsal I want you to get up. It's hard to just watch, you have to get up and do it, but you also have to be respectful of the other Actors' process and give a little space if needed. Once we start Tech, I always tell the Swings to get on the stage and look at the numbers, look at the spike marks, be in the Wings and watch where everybody is going. If it's allowed, and a lot of the time it is, I suggest they take their breaks a little earlier so they can use the stage while the rest of the cast is on break. Also during Tech, my lighting calls with the lighting designer are early in the day, and I have the Swings onstage to walk through the show while we light it. That gives them more time onstage, plus the producers pay them extra.

What are your expectations for a Swing once the show is up and running?

For every show, I have a bible—all the Choreography is notated, the staging is blocked out, there are maps [or charts] showing where props or chairs should be, character breakdowns and Tracking Sheets are included. The bible stays in the Stage Management office and it's mainly for the Associate to refer to, however the Actors and Swings use it too. The responsibility for pulling together all that information falls to the Associate, like Tara Young or Chris Peterson or Jeff Whiting, but really everyone contributes. Today, however, the way these bibles are made has been revolutionized by an app called Stage Write that was created by Jeff Whiting. It's being used by Broadway shows, Disney, Universal, Cirque du Soleil, and more. People can compare notes and share information, which is fantastic. It's a much easier, more efficient way to create a bible. And for the Swings, it allows them to see overhead shots of the Blocking and Choreography, plus it separates out every single Track in the show. Almost all of the Swings and Dance Captains I work with use Stage Write. Aside from the bible, the Swings really just have to be prepared for anything. I know some shows allow Swings to leave the theatre a little early if things are going well. I remember during *Contact*, it had been a smooth night, no one was out, and Angelique Ilo was all set to go home. Just as the music began to play for the curtain call, one of the dancers injured her knee. And there was Angelique in her street clothes, bag on her shoulder, car keys in hand—she threw everything down and ran onstage just as she was. The Choreography in the curtain call is all partnering and she knew someone would be without a partner. She could get away with it because the costumes in the curtain call are a mix of period and contemporary, but the point is she was ready to go at a moment's notice and didn't hesitate for even a second. You just have to be prepared for absolutely anything.

What would hinder a person from being a good Swing?

For some people, it can be a part of their personality that keeps them from thinking fast enough or they have an anxiety level that I see onstage, or the backstage traffic overwhelms them. Some Swings can replicate exactly what they're supposed to, and other

Swings are able to go onstage and wing it and it works out fine. And, if they wing it and get away with it, then that's okay with me. But I can tell when a Swing is overwhelmed, even if she's hitting the right marks. You can't be in this position and be easily overwhelmed because that's when things go wrong and someone gets hurt. You have to stay cool under pressure, and that's something I look for during auditions.

What do you do if a Swing doesn't seem to be working out?

I'm always happy to talk to a Swing if I feel something isn't right. If our chat goes well then I'll allow him another opportunity to go on. But if the problem is consistent, then I'd rather redistribute tracks instead of firing someone. I'll talk to the other Swings to find out if they're comfortable taking on more. Shuffling things around or making him a second cover will give the Swing more time to learn it. And there are times when you notice a Swing just isn't right for a certain role. You assign tracks early on, and later you think, "Hmm, now that I see him, that Swing might be better for that other track." In that case, you sit down and have a conversation about it, and usually people are fine. But if I see someone is struggling then I have to recognize it and find a way to solve it.

How do you deal with the Swings' costumes being made last, even though they may have to go on before Opening?

During rehearsals and Tech, I'm always checking with the Wardrobe department to find out where we are with the Swings' costumes. Sometimes Management won't approve building all the Swing costumes until we're already in Previews, so it's important to stay on top of the situation. I want to make sure there's a plan for getting someone dressed and onstage, even if a specific costume isn't ready, and just asking that question is usually enough to get everyone thinking about the problem. I also feel it's essential that all Swings have a chance to move in their costumes. More so than the dance steps or the Blocking or the props, it's being unfamiliar with what you're wearing that can throw you off. The Choreography might feel different if you've never tried it in a sequined vest or in your new pants. And if it's a new musical you're working on, numbers are constantly changing and scenes are being added or cut, so you really have to follow up to make sure all departments know who needs what.

How do you feel about putting Swings on in order for them to "get their feet wet" or if their family is in town?

That's a complicated question. Traditionally, it's not something I'm in favor of. However, I feel it might be okay if the show has been running for a while. But if the show is gearing up for Tony voters, or preparing for critics, or if the Principals are less inclined to change it up like that, then I would rather not pull an Actor out of the show just to put on a Swing. Again, there are a lot of factors that would go into that decision, but generally speaking, I would say no if I feel it would be more disruptive than helpful.

If a Swing wanted to move into the Regular Playing Company, what would you say?

That happened to Jim Borstelmann during the run of *The Producers*. One of the Ensemble members was leaving and Jim made it clear to me that he wanted to be in the show. If a Swing tells me he wants to move into the show, it sticks in my mind. It was obvious to me how talented and funny Jim is, so when the opportunity came up, the stars aligned, and it was the right Track for Jim and he was absolutely fantastic in that spot. Of course the most famous Swing story is Brad Oscar's. When we were casting *The Producers*, I wanted to hire Brad to swing. At the time, he was playing Santa Claus in Branson and I think he was initially reluctant to leave. Before opening on Broadway, the show went to Chicago, where the Actor playing Franz Liebkind injured his knee and Brad ended up playing the part for most of the run. When we came back to New York, the role officially became Brad's and he was nominated for a Tony Award. And a year later his name was above the title and he was playing Max Bialystock on Broadway. That's one of those wonderful stories in which an Actor is hesitant to swing, but I recognized what a great comic performer Brad is and I was determined to get him out of that Santa Claus suit in the Midwest and into our show. I had no idea his journey would be so successful.

What is your advice for a Swing that has just been hired?

I would say absorb everything around you. Observe not just what you're told to, but take in everything around you. Pay attention to how the show is created. It takes a village to create a musical and it's a miracle when a musical actually gets up and running. To create a musical where there never was a musical before is an amazing experience to be part of and something you'll never forget. So go in with a positive attitude and be ready to absorb it all. Go in with a positive attitude, knowing that you were chosen because you are smarter and better, not because you are less.

SUSAN STROMAN (Director/Choreographer of over fifteen Broadway shows)

Jerry Mitchell

What was your first professional job as a Swing?

A Chorus Line, National Tour 1980. I was in college at Webster University in the conservatory and was offered the tour when the show was auditioning in St. Louis. I went on the road for ten weeks over the summer before going to NYC to do my first Broadway show, *Brigadoon*, where I was also an understudy to John Curry.

What was your next Swing job and what was your process like?

I came to New York, and I did *Brigadoon*, and when *Brigadoon* was closing I got hired to do *Woman of the Year* with Lauren Bacall. I got hired as a Swing. It was my second Broadway show, swinging eight guys. I was the first Swing they hired. Ed Nolfi, the Assistant to the Choreographer, was actually there but only if they needed him. He had never gone on and the show had just opened. I went on a lot for those guys: Michael Kubala, Sergio Cal, Robert Warners . . . I went on quite a bit for them, and I did that for six months. After *Woman of the Year*, I swung *Barnum*. That was my third Broadway show and the second time being a Swing. Joe Layton had tried to hire me for something else, so he hired me for this Swing position, because I could tap dance and hold a guy standing on my shoulders, and I could ride a unicycle. Everything else I had to learn. I had to learn how to juggle balls, pins, boxes and rings, walk on a high wire, do the teeterboard, walk on painter stilts . . . I had to learn to do everything. I do not ever remember having a book, or cards, or notes. I must have had one, but I don't remember it. I don't ever remember writing that stuff down. When I became Assistant on shows I kept detailed books of everything. I was very much a champion for the Swings because, having done it myself, I knew what a hard and important job it was.

How did you like being a Swing?

For me, the hardest part of being a Swing was knowing where to be without having rehearsal with the cast. Patterns, steps, and Blocking were easy to do and remember. Having the time with the other Actors was the hard part, because it was usually not going to happen. *Barnum* was the first show where it was completely bizarre to swing because they were all individuals. And rarely did they ever do anything that was a Chorus number, where each person was doing the exact same thing. I even covered women in that show, so it was very strange. And each person had a different talent. Like one person was a juggler, one person was a clown, one person did the high wire, one person did stilts, and one person was a tap dancer. So they each had their own sort of specialty, and I had none of that experience beforehand. I had to learn that all in two weeks in circus school. And it was harrowing, because I was the least confident in that job.

How did you deal with that anxiety?

Practice. Practice. Practice. Particularly [in] *Barnum*, because you're dealing with physical feats. We had to do the teeter boards. We practiced every single day. We would get there about an hour and a half before the show [and] the stage was open. We'd do the teeter boards, we'd do the high wire, we'd do all that stuff. A lot of the people in that show had learned it specifically for that show and had become quite accomplished. And then there were other people who were circus performers, so they were always there to help you and teach you. So it was a great job to do because I can juggle now, I can juggle anything.

How do you think the role of a Swing has changed over the years?

Well, I think it's changed because I think much more is required of Swings—as is required of [all] Ensemble members. Ensembles used to sing, dance, OR act . . . sometimes you didn't do all three. My first Broadway show, *Brigadoon*, was in 1980. So much has changed in a Broadway show since then. And I was a baby; I was twenty years old stepping on the stage. I was in the dancing Chorus of *Brigadoon*. I also sang, but there were people hired specifically to be singers and not dance. And then there were people who were hired specifically to play smaller roles, and they were older people playing fathers and mothers who did a little bit of dancing—a lot more singing, but certainly were neither a singing Chorus or a dancing Chorus. They were sort of a small role/specifically cast. That was the first show I did that was that way, and that was the last show I did that was that way. I mean

I came right at the crux of that time when everything was trying to get condensed down to cut the running cost of a Broadway show. As the running costs go down, the demands on every performer go up. And the caliber of the actual talent that they bring to the piece has to increase, to be hired. It's the same for Swings. I often now have to find Swings who can go on and not just sing and dance, but actually play small parts—because they're covering four or five small parts. And my show, *Kinky Boots*, is a real dilemma because it's not a Chorus. I've got six angels who sing and dance one way, and then I've got five or six factory worker guys who are completely different in look/style/ability and then it's the same thing with the women. So, I've got a young set and an older set who have to be covered, and can't be covered by the same person. It's very difficult. And, of course, I'm directing and choreographing the show, I have to try to keep the running costs down because I understand the economics of the theatre today.

What are you looking for, when hiring your potential Swings?

I look at how quickly they learn, how accurately they learn, and how calm they are in the process. Their ability to learn quickly is a necessity. Speed is my number one test. Specifically, if I'm looking for Swings, I go fast.

Do you think there is any correlation in Swings moving up to Dance Captain, Assistant, and then Choreographer positions?

A lot of my Swings become my Assistants. It happens. I mean, Rusty [Mowery] was my Swing and now he's my Assistant. Often, my Swings want to get to the next place and be an Assistant. They don't want to be in the show, they actually want to help me set the show and then move on to set multiple Companies or a Company that I'm not involved with.

Do you like to hire one of your Swings as your Dance Captain?

Always, if possible. Because usually they learn quickly, and usually they have a great temperament. I'm looking for someone who can work with a lot of different personalities and not get flustered; keep an even-keeled production while I'm away from it.

Sometimes other cast members don't always understand how hard the job of a Swing can be. How do you deal with members of the cast that can be . . . tricky?

By doing a good job and ignoring *that* personality.

What do you expect from your Swings?

I expect them to be brilliant. I really do. I expect them to be on it, with no rehearsal. Literally, they have to be ready to be thrown in. Because nine times out of ten, you're on in a moment's notice and that's it. I know, *I was a Swing too*!! Maybe you get an hour onstage to run three numbers before you have to perform them . . . maybe, if you're lucky. What I have tried to do in the past, is right from the start, with my Swings, I say, "You're not sitting down. You're up, you're in the back, you're learning it, and when these people go to their costume fittings, I don't want to see any empty spaces. You're in. The best way to do it is to get in it. Get in it while it's being built. Don't wait. And don't worry so much about taking your notes, until I tell you the number's set. Because you're just going to be rewriting, and rewriting, and rewriting. And you're doing 'that' instead of doing 'this.' So look, learn, get up on your feet, do it in the back." In *Catch Me if You Can*, my two [female Swings] Sarah [Andreas] and Kristin [Piro] . . . those girls were unbelievable. They were there every day, before rehearsal for at least thirty to forty-five minutes. They were always working on their lunch hour. That's what I do. I'm always there an hour before, I'm working on lunch hour . . . and they both worked in Pre-Production with me. I almost always invite the Swings into Pre-Production with me.

How would you deal with a Swing asking to join the Regular Playing Company, if a slot becomes available?

I don't have a problem with that. You've earned it, really. But you have to fit the Track. You really have to fit the Track. And sometimes a Swing doesn't completely fit *one* Track, they can play many Tracks, but they're actually 90 percent of that Track, or 78 percent of that Track because they also are 26 percent of the other Track, and 32 percent of that Track . . . so sometimes they're not exactly right for the part. But they're very close.

Have you had any resistance from Producers when discussing the number of Swings?

With *Kinky Boots* I said, "This is it. This is what I have to start with to make this show work." They tried to talk me down and I said, "No, I can't do that. It will jeopardize the well-being of the show. This is what I know I will need to keep the show running."

Do you include your Swings in publicity for the show?

I always include the Swings in the television shows, and the recordings. I've never actually had a Producer say no to me yet when I've brought that up. Usually when I bring that up, with the Producers I've worked with, they say, "Yeah, that's a great idea." And they agree to it. Which makes me understand that they understand the value of the job that's being done. I've never worked on a show that hasn't done that. I've been fortunate. Or maybe I've made that known to Producers from the start. So that's probably the difference. Maybe because I was one.

What advice would you give to someone who was just cast as a Swing?

Watch, and get on your feet and do. Don't just sit and take notes. And ask questions! Because when you actually do go on in a spot, there are a lot of little things that you don't have time to see. It's not just what's happening onstage, it's what's happening backstage. That's why Swings are so valuable to me. I've always been inclusive of them. So I've never excluded them—I've thought of Swings as a necessity to the health of the production. Not an expense. It's just a no-brainer. And I think that everyone that works with me, sort of knows that's how I treat them.

> JERRY MITCHELL (Director/Choreographer of over thirteen Broadway shows; Swing on *Barnum*, *Woman of the Year*, *Brigadoon*)

Rob Ashford

You've worked quite a bit in London. Are there any differences in the job overseas?

It is so different in England—the perception of Swings and everything. Swings here are valued, and are usually some of the best people. And over there, they're like second-class citizens, they're "below stairs." I try to instill in them that it's the opposite. It's an important position. I was a Swing in most of the Broadway shows I was in. The best people are the Swings, not the worst people.

What was your first Swing experience?

I moved to [New York City] and on my first show I was the Swing on *Anything Goes* at Lincoln Center. That was a LORT theatre; on LORT [contracts] you didn't have to have Swings. I made it to the end of the audition, and I felt really good that I was going to get it, and then I didn't get it. So I was very upset. And then, the show opened and got these rave reviews, and I was so depressed because I really thought that I was going to get that. And the day after the opening when all those rave reviews were in all the papers, they called from Lincoln Center and said, "We'd love for you to join the Company as our Swing. Come tonight and watch the show." In the audition, they had this girl named Amy O'Brien and me in line to do that. They had planned that if the show was a success, and they were going to run, they would know they needed Swings and they were just going to call us. And they also made me the Assistant Dance Captain—once I had been there for a little bit.

Did anyone teach you how to swing?

Alice Oakes was the Dance Captain, and she had been a Swing before. She taught a lot of dance. She was really good and patient, and really good about explaining it. I don't know why, it just came naturally. It wasn't an issue. I was a good student, always organized. I made my book, and I still have my book. I had to do it for me. For example when I'm taking notes, when I make a mistake I don't erase it. I mark through something and I leave it like that. Those little mark-throughs, the X'es, are something I would tie in, so I would remember it. If I typed out something on a computer, that would mean nothing to me. It doesn't do me any good. I would do colors. Everyone would have a different color, and I would match the color to the personality. And I could just see the colors in my head. I didn't do little notebooks or flip books, just the big bible. And all I would [think] is, "I'm on for you tonight and you're red." Then I would think through "red" in my head.

What other shows did you Swing?

I did the production of *The Most Happy Fella* at the Booth theatre (the two-piano version), where I was the Swing. And, then my next Swing job was *My Favorite Year* at Lincoln Center, where I was the Swing and the Dance Captain. It was a fraught show. But . . . you learn a lot. That's where I really learned a whole lot about making a show (making changes and all of those kinds of things). It was a good learning experience! It was very informative. Then I went into *Crazy for You*, where I actually wasn't a Swing or a Dance Captain. Then I went on tour with *Kiss of the Spider Woman*, where I was Swing and Dance Captain; and then I came back and did *Victor/Victoria*, where I was Swing and Dance Captain; and then I did *Parade* at Lincoln Center where I was the Assistant Choreographer and Swing/Dance Captain.

How did it feel, going from being a Swing in a couple shows, to having your own track?

I was bored to tears. *Crazy for You* was hard, but I think my body held up better doing *Crazy for You* than it did swinging. I knew what I was doing every show. I could warm up. I never had to be thrown on. Even though when you're swinging, sometimes you get to rest, it was better for my body doing eight shows a week.

Do you think there is a connection to Swings moving up to Dance Captain, then Assistant, then to become Choreographers?

I guess it's the natural progression, if you have an inkling of the talent. For Swings, someone sees in you, at that audition, a certain . . . thing. A certain sharpness or quickness (especially if it's someone new that you don't know), [is] why they always get pegged. Because good Swings are impossible to find, they are a rarity. That's why you say to people, "It's not a punishment. It's just because you do it so well!"

Do you prefer an Offstage or Onstage Dance Captain?

I prefer someone offstage to be the Dance Captain. I think it's better. I think that I was always offstage when I was Dance Captain. [In] *Crazy for You*, the Dance Captain was onstage. The only people who got notes were the people around her. And yes, she would sit out once a week to watch the whole thing, but it's not the same. As a Swing/Dance Captain you are popping into all the different tracks. You go, "Oh, I never knew that. . . . It's crazy there but over here it's so different." You realize it because you're in it. It's a good thing. I do think that's the best way. Actually, I think that the best way is to have a Dance Captain offstage, and the Assistant [Dance Captain] onstage. I do think that's the absolute best. Because then you have someone who's in there every night doing it, who starts sensing some things—the morale or the mood or whatever. And they come to whatever partnering rehearsals and things like that. I find that [to be] the best.

How do you think the job has changed over the years?

Well, I feel like the one thing that's changed is that you get paid a lot more for it now than you used to, so that's good. I feel like the worth of the job is appreciated more . . . I think. I think the basic job is probably the same. I think that people today, in a show, do the same thing I did in *Anything Goes*. Different shows, same job. I don't think that's changing. I think the basic job will stay the same.

How do you go about selecting your Swings in an audition, especially if they've never swung before?

The Swing pile . . . probably three things go into the Swing pile. Now these are Swings for a big new show, or a big revival. I'm saying that because when the show's already running, you get pickier about it. You're trying to kind of fit people into it. I'm talking about a big new show. You get into the Swing pile when you, Number One, have done it before and it's on [your] resumé. That's one thing that helps guide you to that pile, because, you know how to do that specific job in the show. Number Two would be the singing. Generally the Swings are the better singers, of the dancers particularly. So when you're sitting there, trying to figure things out, and someone comes in and sings really great, then quite often the Musical Director or I will write "Swing" because they sing well. Number Three would be sharpness; being calm in the room and not panicking with the partnering. Particularly in partnering, because people can get super stressed because they don't know how to share. They're, like, so used to being on their own, that when they are partnered with someone else, they tense up. So I would say I'm looking for a calmness, a confidence, and also someone who picks up quickly.

What is your relationship to Swings, now that you're a Director/Choreographer?

I still have a good relationship with the Swings. I really appreciate [them] and I rarely ever worry. I kind of look forward to seeing the show with the Swings in it. I think that sometimes you add that one other new energy and it kind of throws the ball back up into the air, in a way that makes you see something different. I kind of like it.

Do you try to make sure anything specific is provided for the Swings?

Like a Swing table? Yeah, I'm very strict about that. It's got to be a proper Swing Tech table, in the right position in the theatre for all of the Tech. That's one thing I do. The other thing I do, (and I learned it in London because they all do that) [is to ask that] Swings must have all of their costumes [on the] first day of Tech, just like all of the cast. "No, we can't wait and do them later, no." And I always insist that the Swings do the Tony [Award]s, and the [Macy's Thanksgiving Day] Parade, and the [cast] Album . . . because I remember feeling like such a second-class citizen, in *Anything Goes*, when they were making the album and they weren't going to use the Swings (and they probably didn't want to include us because we weren't great singers, for one). But I remember being quite hurt about it and actually saying something to Stage

Management. I think I said something about [it] to Patti [LuPone], and then sure enough we were going to do it. And not only that, but when they started doing the tap recordings, they had the whole cast doing the tapping in the *Anything Goes* number. It was chaotic. So they decided they would only do it with four people, and double it. And the two Swings were chosen. We were chosen because, not only were we good tappers, but mainly because we had been cleaned the most. We knew it the right way, because we had been taught it that way. I remember that one of the divas in the cast was kind of over the fact that we were chosen to do the tapping on the album, and they weren't. But, the Swings are a complete member of the Company and they should always be treated that way, on every occasion.

What is it like for the Creative Team when a Swing has to be thrown on in Previews?

No matter how great your Swings are or how much you love them, in that part of the promotion of the show, when you're putting it all out there, it's all so delicate that you just want everybody [in the Regular Playing Company] to be there—the people that you've been in the room with. They're not messing it up. It just draws your attention in a way it shouldn't. I think that's amazingly hard, and it's the worst period of time. But I would say to a Swing (and I think that's what I did as a Swing), use that time. Think of that Preview period as your major work time—not that your major work happens after the opening. I would grab a bite to eat and then get right back on the stage, every Preview. Just keep up, and get with your Swing partners and assign first and second covers and really rally together. Don't be put off because things keep changing. I think that everyone will have that moment when you're creating your book and you're ready to go, and then it changes. Then you start again, and it changes. And you start again, and it changes. And then you think, "I'm just going to wait." But then, panic really sets in because you really can't wait to do it. It's all of those things. I think it would probably be appropriate to ask the Choreographer if you could come in early, when you know that creating is going on. You know that we're all getting together [the Creative Team] from 9:00–11:00 a.m, to work on the new section and then later we teach the changes to the cast. So I totally don't mind to have another body. I'm happy to have that. I'm happy if someone wants to come in. Then you're in the room when it's being made up. And then, at least when it's being taught, you're ahead of the game. I think that during the rehearsal process you have a feeling that you're not needed at this time, when you are really needed at this time. Make yourself available. See if you're needed . . . then you will always feel more a part of everything.

How do you feel about someone asking to move into the Ensemble?

I think it's absolutely fine to ask. As long as you're willing to take the "no." You do have to understand what a difficult decision that is, for the Creative Team. From all the rehearsals to teach all the tracks, to the costumes. . . . Now if it's a show like *How to Succeed* with so many people coming and going, and so many people being taught, and so many people waiting in the Wings . . . then come to me and say, "You know I'd like to go into _____'s spot." Then I'm like, "Okay, we could bring in this guy to do that. And then maybe 'so and so' could do that." and I'm like, "Okay, yeah!" I'm certainly all for it—for being honest and asking. But also try to understand when I say no.

If someone were hired as a Swing for the very first time, what advice would you give them?

I would say, whatever you do, try to get a really good, strong, and positive relationship going with the Dance Captain, Stage Management, and the other Swings. I would certainly do that. Because I think that is your family that you have the most contact with, and I think that it's a really important relationship. It's your support. Then you can get help, you won't feel alone, and you have support . . . and I think that's really important.

How would you improve the life of a Swing or Dance Captain?

Well, I would always suggest for the Dance Captain, that when you put in extra work (because the overtime payment is minimal), work out with your Management that you accrue extra hours and time that you can bank, and then maybe have a night off here or there. That's something I did in *Victor/Victoria*, because I was rehearsing every minute of every day—twenty-five Replacements in six months. So you say, "Okay don't pay me the $25. Can I just accrue that hour, and then can I have a night that I don't have to be in the building?" Not a night that I'm going to go to Fire Island. I'm talking about, "Okay, I'm going to be at the movie theatre, and you have my number, and if something goes crazy [call me]. . . . Or I'm just going to go have dinner with my boyfriend tonight. Or I'm going to go see another show." And it wasn't like I was not there—I was close by. "You know if you need me, I'm around. And if you need me, call me . . . or text me." So I think that's one thing.

And then that would encourage people to put in the extra time. I mean if Sarah O'Gleby is putting in three new people, then why can't the Swings say, "Why don't I come in? I'll do the partnering. I'll put in that extra time." Of course, Management would say, "No we don't need you," because they're not going to pay you. But what if you could accrue the hours to get a little extra off time? That would be great. And you'll feel more a part of the Company and you also get to know the new cast members, and they're getting to know you, because you dance with them.

So, I think the thing that makes a Swing's life easier is to constantly let them know how special they are and do anything you can, perk-wise, to make that happen. Anytime there are little extra perks, I think they deserve it. (Now I know with the Favored Nations contracts of the world, they can't actually give you more money than is required. And it's not like you will get a massage when no one else does.) I think that other kinds of perks you could do [are] . . . if you have extra dressing rooms in the theatre, I think give the Swings a "Swing room." Not that it's their dressing room. It's hugely important that you're in there with everybody . . . it's about being a part of, not pulling away. But what if you have your own room where you just want to go on a Saturday matinee? You don't want to sit in the dressing room. You want to go read that book, or do something like watch a movie . . . you have a special little place. That doesn't cost anybody anything. Those kinds of little things, anything extra—it is important that Management, the Director, and the Choreographer keep everybody feeling a part of the big picture. Like [at] the Tonys, all of our Swings were on, and they should have been. And yes, it costs more money, but it's important to the success of the show.

ROB ASHFORD (Director/Choreographer of over nine
Broadway shows; Swing on *The Most Happy Fella*,
My Favorite Year, *Parade*, *Victor/Victoria*, *Anything Goes*)

13

Swinging On

So, where do we swing from here? Will Swings start to gain more respect from audiences (and Producers/Management)? We hope so! Will Swings advocate for more advances and protections for themselves in the Production Contract? We hope so! Will technology help Swings to fulfill their duties more efficiently—thanks to Stage Write and Scene Partner (along with other advances)? We know so! Will Swings continue to save the day, save the show, and be heroes for Broadway? You betcha!

Thoughts from the Swings on the Future of Swinging

As Producers attempt to spend less and less to put up a Broadway show, the role of Swing has become a more demanding position. I used to see twice as many Swings on shows that require heavy dancing and singing, but recently these productions are only hiring one male and one female Swing. Each Swing is required to carry both the singing and dancing tracks; this increases the amount of tracks covered by each Swing and also makes internal swinging a requirement from the Company. Moving forward, Swings will be covering both Principal and Ensemble tracks, making them the most impressive members of the Company. I hope we are going to see Actors' Equity step in with more support for these hard-working cast members to ensure they are properly compensated for what is becoming a complicated job.

SARA EDWARDS (Associate/Assistant on two
Broadway shows; Swing on *Follies*)

I think the biggest change, and one that will continue is the use of the Universal Swing across multiple companies. That will only continue for those shows that continue to send out Production tours. What Producers don't realize is that between Companies (and depending on the Creative Team that set that version), things can be wildly different, and so you aren't just doing the same thing, you have to learn a new version of the show.

BRIAN COLLIER (*Mary Poppins,*
Cats—National Tour)

Over the past few years, I've seen the role of a Swing and the lines that define our job become blurred. Swings have been asked to jump between genders and cover as many as twenty different roles, which I think is absolutely ludicrous, especially seeing what the Equity increment is for our job. As a Swing, I have been asked to fill in for Principal roles, that I do not cover, in rehearsals and expected to know material that I am in no way responsible for. In this case, I hope that AEA takes a step forward for Swings and demands a more suitable pay scale for the amount of tracks we cover, as well as defining whether or not it is fair to cross gender or contract lines. It is in our nature, as performers, to want to [go] above and beyond for the love of our profession. But we have to be wary that it doesn't impinge on us, contractually. Hopefully in the next ten years, shows will hire more Swings for every show, so that all roles and responsibilities can be covered without compromising or leaning too heavily on the Swings in the show.

NATHAN PECK (*Kinky Boots, Dance of the Vampires,*
Wicked—Chicago Company)

I think what's happening is the commitment level of the Ensemble and Company has tapered off. Meaning, people don't push through the show with injuries, aches, and pains as much as they used to. I've definitely noticed this over the years. And I think that's basically been great for Swings, because you need more of them. The Swings have definitely gotten better at their craft, both acting and dancing. Previously, Swings were strictly dancer positions. Now you see more Swings also covering Principal roles. I believe the talent pool has gotten better and I've also noticed [that] some people prefer to swing.

CLIFFORD SCHWARTZ (Stage Manager of over thirteen Broadway shows)

Right now performing as a Swing is seen as a doorway to getting the bigger jobs for newer performers. It is not, however, seen as something valuable to established performers. To make it more desirable to work harder than everyone else and receive little to no praise, they should increase the salaries and guarantee first cover for certain roles.

PRESTON ELLIS (*Grease*—First National Tour)

Our Final Thoughts

We hope that Swings will fight for (and receive) more recognition and respect, perhaps reflected in:

- Higher salaries.

- Guaranteed appearances on cast albums, Tony Awards, etc.

- Cap on the number of tracks a Swing can cover.

- Limitations on cross-gender swinging.

- Permission for Swings to have access to archival footage to maintain their bibles.

- MP3s of each Ensemble vocal part made available to the Swings.

- Technologies provided for Swings that will enable them to better fulfill their duties.

Ultimately we know this—as long as Broadway shows continue, there will always be a need for qualified Swings. And, we hope this book will be a helpful tool for all Swings-to-be. The Great White Way is depending on you!

If you ever find yourself cast as a Swing, we hope that you will be proud! Know that others have been where you are and know *exactly* what you are going through. (Sometimes, just knowing that makes the job so much easier.)

To all those who have already made their mark in this noble profession, we congratulate you, honor you, and thank you. You are our heroes!

And, no matter who you are, the next time you see a Broadway show, look through your Playbill and find the Swings. Whether they are on or not, take a moment to recognize their hard work and contribution to the production. Without them, that hit show you are seeing might not survive. Salute the Swings! And, hey, if you are dropping by the stage door, tell them "Great Job" or ask for an autograph—it will make their day—and boy, do they deserve it!

Appendix A: Meet the Swings

The Cast of Swings

Thank you—to all of these fabulous Swings who completed surveys, were interviewed, or submitted their stories for this book! Due to word limits, we were unable to use quotes from all who contributed. But, nonetheless, we thank you and we salute you!

Dara Adler
Meredith Akins
Alicia Albright
Clyde Alves
Rob Ashford
Julie Barnes
Christina Belinsky
Kristine Bendul
Michael Biren
Timothy Bish
Andrew Black
Candi Boyd
Colin Bradbury
Brad Bradley
Stacey Lynn Brass
James Brown III
Todd Buonopane
Kristin Carbone
Darren Carnall
Alexis Carra
Callie Carter
Paula Leggett Chase

Karl Christian
Brian Collier
Chris Copeland
Lucy Costelloe
Patti D'Beck
Bradley Dean
Angela Decicco
Jason DePinto
Michael DeVries
Sarah Dickens
Philipp Dietrich
Kurt Domoney
Jennifer Dunne
Elizabeth Earley
Beverly Edwards
Sara Edwards
Zak Edwards
David Eggers
Preston Ellis
Brooke Leigh Engen
Harvey Evans
AJ Fisher

Merwin Foard
Jenifer Foote
Jennie Ford
Andrew Frace
Drew Franklin
Kurt Froman
Romain Frugé
Larry Fuller
Lisa Gajda
Anthony Galde
Gregory Garrison
Lydia Gaston
Mary Giattino
Greg Graham
Justin Greer
Florian Hacke
Tripp Hanson
Ben Hartley
Cynthia Leigh Heim
John Hillner
Seán Martin
    Hingston

Mark S. Hoebee
Leah Horowitz
Mary Jane Houdina
Nicola Humphrey
JoAnn M. Hunter
Karen Hyland
Holly Hylton
Angelique Ilo
Reginald Holden
   Jennings
Lisa Kassay
Matthew J. Kilgore
Grasan Kingsberry
Michelle Kittrell
Ed Kresley
Mary Ann Lamb
Gina Lamparella
Brandon Leffler
Ian Liberto
Synthia Link
Rosemary Loar
Kevin C. Loomis
Sean MacLaughlin
Joanne Manning
Richie Mastascusa
Sean McKnight
Jessica McRoberts

Joseph Medeiros
Jerry Mitchell
Betsy Morgan
Lee Morunga
Sarah O'Gleby
John O'Hara
Marc Oka
Nathan Peck
Jody Reynard
Clinton Roane
Stephen Roberts
Arbender J.
   Robinson
Janet Saia
Rommy Sandhu
Eric Santagata
Mark Santoro
Jonalyn Saxer
Nathan Scherich
Jenny Schlensker
Eric Sciotto
Michael James Scott
Brian Shepard
Jeff Siebert
Megan Sikora
Matthew Sipress
Jason Snow

Lisa Sontag
Tony Stevens
Sam Strasfeld
Kelly Sullivan
Colin Trahan
Allyson Turner
   (Wilkerson)
Melanie Vaughan
Nicky Venditti
Jerome Vivona
Michelle O'Steen
   Vivona
Josh Walden
Matt Wall
Mimi B. Wallace
Thom Christopher
   Warren
Tonya Wathen
Patrick Wetzel
Jeff Williams
Jamaal Wilson
Emma Woods
Katrina Yaukey
Courtney Young
Samantha Zack
Deone Zanotto

Appendix B: Sources/Further Reading

New York Public Library for the Performing Arts
(Programs and Clippings Archive)
40 Lincoln Center Plaza
New York, NY 10023
Available online: http://www.nypl.org (accessed: May 2014).

Actors' Equity Association
(Document Library)
Available online: http://www.actorsequity.org (accessed: August 2014).

Internet Broadway Database
Available online: http://www.ibdb.com (accessed: August 2014).

Stage Write Software
Available online: http://www.stagewritesoftware.com (accessed: August 2014).

Scene Partner App
Available online: http://www.scenepartnerapp.com (accessed: August 2014).

Index